T0299235

Work Organizational Reforms and Employment Relations in the Automotive Industry

General Motors (GM)'s attempt to adapt the renowned Toyota production system for its own automotive manufacturing plants had historically produced disappointing results. Why was it not sufficiently successful? This book aims to shed insights into GM's failed attempt through the analysis of work organization reforms and labor–management relations on production-system efficiency.

The book examines collective bargaining agreements between automakers and the United Auto Workers union and the arbitration rulings in retrospect to illuminate the critical role continuous improvement activities initiated by production workers would play in enhancing performance management. It also looks at the impact of the meritocratic system in Japanese auto plants on performance success. As GM begins operations at its new electric vehicle assembly plant, Factory Zero, the book analyses the challenges of such production for both employment relations and workforce deployment.

The book will be a useful reference for those interested in a comparative study of management styles and a better understanding of Japanese manufacturing practices.

Kenichi Shinohara is Professor at the Division of Business Administration, Kyoto Sangyo University, Japan.

Routledge Focus on Business and Management

The fields of business and management have grown exponentially as areas of research and education. This growth presents challenges for readers trying to keep up with the latest important insights. *Routledge Focus on Business and Management* presents small books on big topics and how they intersect with the world of business research.

Individually, each title in the series provides coverage of a key academic topic, whilst collectively, the series forms a comprehensive collection across the business disciplines.

The Multiple Case Study Design
Methodology and Application for Management Education
Daphne Halkias, Michael Neubert, Paul W. Thurman and Nicholas Harkiolakis

Organizations, Strategic Risk Management and Resilience
The Impact of Covid-19 on Tourism
Patrizia Gazzola, Enrica Pavione and Ilaria Pessina

Organizations and Complex Adaptive Systems
Masha Fidanboy

Managing Complexity in Healthcare
Lesley Kuhn and Kieran Le Plastrier

Work Organizational Reforms and Employment Relations in the Automotive Industry
American Employment Relations in Transition
Kenichi Shinohara

For more information about this series, please visit: www.routledge.com/
Routledge-Focus-on-Business-and-Management/book-series/FBM

Work Organizational Reforms and Employment Relations in the Automotive Industry

American Employment Relations in Transition

Kenichi Shinohara

Routledge
Taylor & Francis Group

LONDON AND NEW YORK

First published 2022
by Routledge
4 Park Square, Milton Park, Abingdon, Oxon OX14 4RN

and by Routledge
605 Third Avenue, New York, NY 10158

Routledge is an imprint of the Taylor & Francis Group, an informa business

© 2022 Kenichi Shinohara

The right of Kenichi Shinohara to be identified as author of this work has been asserted in accordance with sections 77 and 78 of the Copyright, Designs and Patents Act 1988.

All rights reserved. No part of this book may be reprinted or reproduced or utilised in any form or by any electronic, mechanical, or other means, now known or hereafter invented, including photocopying and recording, or in any information storage or retrieval system, without permission in writing from the publishers.

Trademark notice: Product or corporate names may be trademarks or registered trademarks, and are used only for identification and explanation without intent to infringe.

British Library Cataloguing-in-Publication Data
A catalogue record for this book is available from the British Library

Library of Congress Cataloging-in-Publication Data
Names: Shinohara, Kenichi, author.
Title: Work organizational reforms and employment relations in the automotive industry : American employment relations in transition / Kenichi Shinohara.
Description: Milton Park, Abingdon, Oxon; New York, NY: Routledge, 2023. | Series: Routledge focus on business & management | Includes bibliographical references and index. |
Identifiers: LCCN 2022009044 (print) | LCCN 2022009045 (ebook) | ISBN 9781032252704 (hardback) | ISBN 9781032252728 (paperback) | ISBN 9781003282426 (ebook)
Subjects: LCSH: Automobile industry workers--United States. | Automobile industry workers--Japan. | Automobile industry and trade--United States--Personnel management. | Automobile industry and trade--Japan--Personnel management. | General Motors Corporation--Personnel management. | Toyota Jidōsha Kabushiki Kaisha--Personnel management.
Classification: LCC HD8039.A82 U765 2023 (print) | LCC HD8039.A82 (ebook)
| DDC 331.7/62920973--dc23/eng/20220222
LC record available at https://lccn.loc.gov/2022009044
LC ebook record available at https://lccn.loc.gov/2022009045

ISBN: 9781032252704 (hbk)
ISBN: 9781032252728 (pbk)
ISBN: 9781003282426 (ebk)

DOI: 10.4324/9781003282426

Typeset in Times New Roman
by Deanta Global Publishing Services, Chennai, India

Contents

Figures

Tables

Preface

This book describes work organization reform and labor–management relationships in the US auto industry, focusing on the auto plants of General Motors, which has used Toyota as a benchmark. The book is based on research of primary sources and personal interviews.

GM began making efforts to apply the Toyota production system in its plants in the 1980s, but labor–management relationships were unhealthy and reforms were less than successful, and in 2009 GM declared bankruptcy. Following this, reforms in the production system were further accelerated, but improvements in employment relations have been insufficient. In sum, GM's performance management system is not functioning well compared to that of Toyota.

Unlike Toyota, which has a robust internal promotion system—Toyota's current vice president is a former production worker—GM has been unable to bridge the labor–management gap. With the potential work improvement contributions of production workers not being fully utilized, GM plants do not operate smoothly.

Discussion of work organization reform increased in the United States starting in the 1980s, and the "team concept," which is a prominent feature of the Japanese workplace, has attracted much attention. GM has tried to introduce teams modeled on the Toyota production system. The objective of this book is to show why work organization reform has not progressed in the US auto industry as much as hoped for.

Existing research studies on this topic are lacking with regard to the following points:

1) The viewpoint of "performance management" in work organization reform
2) Accurate understanding of work organization in Japan, such as the roles of continuous improvement activities (*kaizen*) and meritocracy for rank-and-file workers

This book considers and explores these points, based on an analysis of primary sources (e.g., labor contracts and arbitration records) and personal interviews. Existing books in English have focused on how "team collaboration" and "autonomy" of production workers can improve factory production efficiency. However, the fact that workers' continuous improvement activities are the basis of "performance management" of the entire plant, and the critical role played by meritocracy in Japanese auto plants, has not been revealed or explained in any English book.

As production workers are key to the success of any manufacturing system based on the Japanese model, cooperative labor–management relations are critical. To understand labor–management relationships in the US auto industry, it is necessary to examine and understand the background behind collective bargaining agreements between the automakers and the United Auto Workers union, as well as arbitration rulings that have helped shape those agreements. This book is the first to describe those agreements and the disputes and discussions that accompany them.

Most of the research activities for this study have been conducted in Michigan. The periods when direct interviews were conducted are noted in the footnotes of each chapter. Outside of the interview period described above, I occasionally visited Michigan to gather materials and information. In addition, I have already written books on this subject in Japanese, but this book is a new version of those books with significant changes, additions, and corrections.

Chapter 1: Achievements and challenges of work organization reform in the US auto industry: An overview of the research

This chapter reviews previous research studies on US work organization reform. Many of these studies focus on Japanese work organization characteristics, such as the "team concept" at Japanese auto plants. However, examinations of performance management in the United States are lacking. This book builds on survey and field research in order to fill the gap left by other studies and elucidate the current state of work organization reform in the US auto industry.

Chapter 2: The development of seniority rights and establishment of rules for job transfer and promotion in the United States: General Motors Corporation

This chapter traces the historical evolution of seniority rights and rules for job transfer and promotion at US auto plants through the 1980s. Traditional "job control unionism" and the seniority system are well known, but the concrete structure and historical background of the seniority system have not been documented in detail until now. Based on an investigation of primary materials, including original arbitration records and past National Agreements between the UAW and GM, this chapter provides a ground-breaking analysis that clarifies the historical development of seniority rules which form the basis of US work organization.

Chapter 3: Work organization reform (1): The case of General Motors Plant A

This chapter examines the reality of work organization up until GM's bankruptcy in 2009. The UAW and GM had discussed large-scale work organization reforms during contract negotiations through the 1990s, with the main topic being changes to the strong seniority system, which presented an obstacle to reform. Based on an analysis of national and local agreement documents and interviews with representatives of labor and management, this chapter describes how the seniority system, which was the basis of traditional job control unionism, was simplified to facilitate the carrying out of reforms. But the reforms made were not enough to prevent GM from filing for bankruptcy in 2009.

Chapter 4: Work organization reform at General Motors (2)

This chapter continues to examine work organization reform. Under the terms of the bankruptcy, GM was obliged to introduce a stronger performance management system on the shop floor. The realities of labor–management confrontation and cooperation concerning performance management and work organization reforms are described, along with attempts to introduce continuous improvement (*kaizen*), product development teams (PDT), and new quality control systems. These reforms set the stage for the development of GM's Global Manufacturing System (GMS), which is described in the next chapter.

Chapter 5: GM's Global Manufacturing System (GMS) and the union

This chapter describes the development of GM's Global Manufacturing System (GMS) and the involvement of the UAW. The GMS is an original GM concept, but it is clearly influenced by Japanese work organization, including Toyota's labor–management consultation system. However, for the GMS to function well, systems and programs involving production workers, such as continuous improvement, a rigorous PDCA (Plan-Do-Check-Action) cycle, and meritocracy and an internal promotion system, are needed. GM and the UAW are continuing to work on these reforms. In recent years, the US auto industry has been forced to adapt to the "EV (Electric Vehicle)." GM is aiming to start operations at its new EV assembly plant, Factory Zero, in 2022. We will analyze the employment and workforce allocation challenges associated with these latest innovations in automobile production.

Chapter 6: Conclusion

This chapter summarizes the content of Chapters 1–5 and offers suggestions regarding employment relations in the US auto industry from the viewpoint of the Japanese employment system.

Acknowledgments

I would like to express my sincere gratitude for the cooperation and guidance I have received from many people. In particular, this book could not have been published without the following people.

First of all, I would like to express my deepest gratitude to Professor Emeritus Mitsuo Ishida of Doshisha University, who has been my advisor since my graduate school days; he is also the co-editor of "The GM Experience," published in Japanese in 2003, and is a leading labor researcher in Japan. I may not always be a good student for him, but I have tried to do my research in my own way until today.

Mr. Mark Strolle, who is now a Program Presenter at Michigan State University School of Human Resources and Labor Relations, has been my most important research collaborator. He is an outstanding professional in the field of US labor–management relations and has held a number of important positions at the UAW, including Representative. I would not have been able to conduct my research without him.

Professor Emeritus Clair Brown of the University of California has provided advice as needed since I was a graduate student to this day. When I was a visiting scholar at the Institute for Research on Labor and Employment at the University of California from 2015 to 2016, she also helped me in many ways.

Mr. Ted Kawashima, Director at Japan Auto Parts Industries Association, has been involved in the automotive industry in Michigan for a long time. His analysis of the US auto industry has been very useful in my research. Apart from his work and research, he is also an expert guitarist, and his talks are always interesting.

I have had the pleasure of talking with Associate Professor Takeshi Sakade of Kyoto University, Professor Emeritus Chirhiro Suematsu of Kyoto University and now of Ritsumeikan University, Professor Hideki Iwaki of Kyoto Sangyo University, and Professor Takashi Hattori of Kyoto University and now of the Ministry of Economy, Trade and Industry. The pleasant conversations with them enriched my often lonely research life. I have been personally indebted to Professor Emeritus Takashi Watanabe of Ritsumeikan University, Associate Professor Akira Tanimoto of Doshisha University, and Professor Tsuyako Nakamura for a long time.

In addition, I continue to receive research stimulation from Dean Keiko Zaima and many other excellent professors at the Faculty of Business Administration, Kyoto Sangyo University, to which I belong.

Last but not least, this book would not have been possible without the cooperation of my wife, Riko, and my daughter, Mizuki, who are part of my life. I would like to take this opportunity to express my sincere gratitude to them.

1 Achievements and challenges of work organization reform in the US auto industry

An overview of the research

Introduction

After the 2008 economic crisis that resulted in General Motors (GM) and Chrysler filing for bankruptcy, Detroit's Big Three automakers began to change their management style. In the past, GM, Chrysler, and Ford had relied on offering financial services to their customers for a significant portion of their profits. GM's financial arm GMAC, for example, provided financing to GM customers and offered mortgages. But in the post-bankruptcy period, the three automakers were forced to focus on their core business of auto manufacturing. Faced with a cash crunch, GM sold 51% of GMAC to the private equity fund Cerberus in 2006 and began making bold efforts to reform management of the production process and improve labor–management relations. Such reform, however, is an ongoing process.

The automobile industry is on the cusp of dramatic change and automakers worldwide are struggling to survive and thrive amid global competition. The intensification of global competition in the auto industry that began in the 1970s is especially interesting from the perspective of employment relations theory. The purpose of this research is to identify and describe the dynamics of work organization at GM, including the company's past and more recent reform efforts.

Toyota, Volkswagen, the Renault–Nissan–Mitsubishi Alliance, and other global automobile manufacturers have continued to reform and improve their production systems in recent decades. General Motors' Global Manufacturing System (GMS) was conceived in 1996 as a management innovation strategy in response to increased global competition. GMS is designed not only to affect the production department directly, but also to enable broader reform in collaboration with other departments, including R&D, sales, purchasing, product design, and engineering, with the aim of improving productivity and product quality. GMS extends not only to other departments within GM, but also to external suppliers. Ultimately, the

DOI: 10.4324/9781003282426-1

United Auto Workers labor union (UAW) has become involved in GMS, further increasing its impact.

In discussing the current international competitiveness of automobile manufacturers, it is necessary to take into account cutting-edge technological innovation in recent years in the areas of electric cars and self-driving vehicles. Another important development is consolidation within the industry and the development of new alliances which include companies outside the industry. These changes have been widely reported in the mass media. However, the degree to which innovative technologies and changing relationships among competitors will be successful cannot be predicted, and as such, these are not suitable for empirical analysis.

In such circumstances, organizational reform at major automobile manufacturers has made considerable progress. The research described in this book focuses on GM's GMS, the cross-plant and cross-region equipment purchasing and integration strategy designed to make GM's global factories more efficient and raise quality levels. Without GMS, it is impossible to understand the reality of GM today. Although GMS spans the entire company, the core of reform takes place in the production department. In the United States, GM management must negotiate labor agreements with the UAW that cover workers' wages, benefits, and conditions of employment. The chapters in this book will analyze the development of GMS, describing its historical development and the structure of GM's work organization, especially with regard to labor–management relations. In order to accurately understand employment relations at the shop floor level, we will analyze the structure and history of work organization at GM, the seniority rule, all arbitration records concerning transfer and promotion, the development of the team concept, and GMS.

Research on American work organizational reform: The case of the automobile industry

This chapter summarizes research published since the 1980s on work organization reform in American automobile plants, identifying trends in work organization reform studies up to the present.

Traditional American labor–management relations are being transformed, and research has been trying to capture these changes. However, few studies have been able to accurately identify and describe the "work rules" of the new order in the workplace. Shinohara (2003) has provided a comprehensive survey of research on work organization reform in the United States from the 1980s to the early 2000s.[1] One of the most prominent themes in this research is the introduction of the "team concept," under which, it is argued, relations between union and management can become more cooperative, and worker satisfaction, autonomy, and motivation can improve. Studies also suggest that implementation of the team concept naturally leads to improvement in productivity and product quality. Is this happy scenario actually true? Is the term "team concept" a magic wand? Based on our research in the US auto industry, we argue that such a view is overly simplistic, naïve, and unsatisfactory: the "team approach" alone does not necessarily have a positive impact on productivity and quality. Also needed is a well-developed and systematic overall scheme, or detailed "master plan."

For example, to truly understand work organization reform in the automobile industry, researchers need to ask and answer questions like these:

- What kind of concrete systems did management introduce to raise the production yield ratio, that is, to increase the yield of satisfactory parts or products that require no repair?
- How, concretely, did management negotiate with and persuade production workers to embrace the system of "build-in-quality?"
- How does the conventional quality control system, that is, the control of quality at the final assembly process, fit in this system?
- What kind of workloads do the production workers accept? Are such workloads semi-compulsory?
- How is the target production yield ratio set, and who sets it?
- How is the PDCA (Plan, Do, Check, Act) cycle carried out? Does it involve production workers?
- How has the role of the quality control manager changed? How did quality control managers react to changes in their power and authority?

In other words, work organization reform that will raise productivity and quality levels requires comprehensive, detailed, and systematic planning and schemes that can achieve targets through the PDCA cycle. It is very difficult for management alone to set appropriate targets and attain them. New work rules are necessary, and agreement and compromise with labor is needed for operations to run smoothly. These are the kind of things that labor researchers must observe and analyze. However, with the exception of a small number of studies described below, these issues have been given little attention.

In the following sections, we take a close look at previous research on work organization reform in US auto plants since the 1980s.

Research trends during the 1980s: A boom in team theory

The goal of workplace reform is to more effectively utilize individual workers' abilities and efforts. Both direct incentives, in the form of wages, and control systems, such as "performance management," "progress management," "management by objectives," and the PDCA cycle, are important in order to maximize workers' contributions.[2]

Wage management reforms undertaken by US automakers since the 1980s were characterized by a "broad-banding of job classifications," which significantly reduced the number of wage and job classifications. This meant that all production workers basically worked for the same wage rate, except for team leaders and skilled trades workers. This situation made it quite difficult to introduce a merit pay system for union members in the US auto industry. In contrast, at auto plants in Japan, a merit system was introduced in the postwar period under which workers' pay is influenced by individual performance.

To be sure, wage system reform in the direction of meritocracy—"pay-for-skill" or "pay-for-knowledge"—has not always been successful. However, most research on the US auto industry pays little attention to the wage system itself, and to the potential benefits of a merit pay system in work organization reform. Researchers' neglect of the wage system is probably due to the fact that "equal pay for equal work" is seen as an unalterable fact of life in the context of adversarial labor relations. The merit pay system in Japanese auto plants, which is very important in motivating production workers, has also received little attention. This is a critical weakness in most research in the field of employment relations in the United States. Shinohara (2003) describes the typical gist of arguments made by American researchers as follows.

> The purpose of work organization change [in the US auto industry] is to make relations between labor and management more cooperative. Changing the traditional approach of job control unionism can raise production workers' skill levels and increase their involvement in decision-making. As a result of this, the organization becomes more efficient and is able to cope with innovation more flexibly, and productivity and quality improve. At the same time, worker autonomy increases and worker job satisfaction increases.[3]

As this quote from Shinohara shows, most research on organization reform in the United States does not investigate or address actual negotiations between labor and management about wages and performance management. Instead, it defaults to the motivational theories of human resources management and organizational behavior.[4]

In the 1980s, the case of NUMMI (New United Motor Manufacturing Inc.) was the focus of numerous research studies. As is well known, NUMMI was originally a GM plant in Fremont, California, which was closed in 1982 and reopened in 1984 as a GM–Toyota joint venture. At NUMMI, Toyota was primarily in charge of production control, and assembled cars were sold under both brands. Important research was conducted on NUMMI, focusing mainly on the team concept on the shop floor, QC (quality control) activities, and the spirit of cooperation among workers in the plant. The success of NUMMI caused many researchers in the United States to become interested in the Toyota production system. But these researchers, for the most part, paid little attention to the "wage management" and "performance management" elements of the Toyota system.

Academic interest in NUMMI is just one example of a "boom" in research about work reorganization that occurred in the 1980s. The essence of most of this research was to argue that things like the "team concept," "flexibility," or "commitment" are associated with improving productivity and quality. Few researchers, however, conducted fieldwork that looked at wage management and performance management systems in detail.

Research trends since the 1990s

Divergence versus convergence

One of the most prominent themes of research and writing on work organization since the 1990s is the question of whether forms of work organization are converging around a single "best" model, or diversifying. The success of Japanese manufacturers in the automobile, electronics, and other industries led some observers to believe that Japanese-style management and production systems were superior in delivering high levels of productivity and quality, and that they would therefore be imitated around the world, with work organizations converging on the "Japanese model." In their book *Converging Divergences* (2000), Katz and Darbishire present an opposing view, arguing that work organization is diverging into four distinct models: the low-wage model, the HRM model, the Japanese model, and the joint-team model.[5] Concerning the four models, they note that:

- The low-wage model is based on traditional management style and does not involve unions.
- The HRM model also does not involve unions; it is focused on a merit wage system and career development of workers.
- The Japanese model includes the elements of merit pay, a seniority wage system, and enterprise unions.

- The joint-team model is characterized by pay-for-performance and semi-autonomous work units. GM's wholly owned subsidiary Saturn is an example of this model.

Katz and Darbishire argue that the diversification of American employment systems is accompanied by increasing employment in the non-union sector, and a divergence in the nature of union versus non-union employment.[6] They also point out that there are great differences from plant to plant in the ways that workers participate in managerial decision-making.

While Katz and Darbishire's divergence argument and classification of work organizations into four models seem reasonable, their work is limited in the degree to which it helps us to understand concretely how productivity and quality are improved. Focusing primarily on the relationship between the weakened union movement and diversification of employment systems, they compare wages and work arrangements between the union and non-union sectors. This is valuable, but it falls short of illuminating exactly how semi-autonomous workgroups improve productivity and quality.

GM's Saturn plant was the first plant in which GM, implementing what it learned from NUMMI, undertook major work organization reform on its own. At Saturn, the character of the work organization tended to be semi-autonomous, but a strict PDCA performance management system was employed to ensure that the goals of improved productivity and quality were met.

Katz and Darbishire classify Saturn's work organization as a joint-team model, characterized by pay-for-performance and semi-autonomous work groups. Such a classification is fine as far as it goes, but what is missing is a more concrete and detailed exploration of exactly how pay-for-performance and semi-autonomous work groups directly result in performance improvements. Greater understanding is needed of the similarities and differences between the joint-team model and the Japanese model, including regarding the characteristics of "teams" in the two models.

Here, we can point out a problem with the word "divergence." "Divergence" is a convenient term for indicating superficial tendencies and characteristics, but it tells us little about many concrete realities and important specifics of work organization. In this book, we present the results of in-depth research into the nature of, and changes in, GM's work organization, with the purpose of illuminating those realities and specifics.

Other research studies, including "United States: Variations on a Theme," by Paul Adler, Thomas A. Kochan, John Paul MacDuffie, Frits K. Pil, and Saul A. Rubinstein, in the book *After Lean Production* (Cornell University Press, 1997), have emphasized divergence as a prominent characteristic of work organization in the United States. In *The Machine*

That Changed the World (Free Press, 1990), James P. Womack, Daniel T. Jones, and Daniel Roos argued that work organization worldwide was converging on the lean production system. However, GM's Wilmington plant, although it adopted lean production, was not able to effectively introduce a team-based work system or job rotation. A lean production system alone is not always enough to improve productivity and quality. While we can agree with Adler et al. that work organization reform in the US auto industry has diverged rather than converging around one model, we believe there is a need to dig more deeply, as there are numerous varieties of work organization at different plants.[7]

To summarize, many researchers in the United States are interested in whether work organization is diverging or converging. Our purpose in this book is to investigate "what those researchers did not research." It goes without saying that workers play a vital role in a firm's production of goods and services, so when management tries to introduce a new work practice policy, it needs to secure the agreement of the workers. Management proposals that would change job tasks call for corresponding changes in wages and treatment of workers, from the union's perspective. That is to say, work organization change also involves changes in union demands, and influences labor–management relations. These changes should be described in detail, something that previous research has not done.

Correctly understanding the Japanese model: Not autonomous teams

While the "divergence of work organization" argument is lacking in specifics about how different models affect productivity and quality, it is nonetheless more sophisticated than much of the discussion around the team concept in the 1980s and early 1990s, which tended toward the naïve belief that when production workers work together as a team, productivity and quality automatically improve. In reality, teams in Japanese work organizations do not always function autonomously, a fact that researchers began to recognize in the latter half of the 1990s. Research studies in the 2000s display a more detailed understanding of Japanese work organization.

In "Leaning toward Teams," a chapter in the 2003 book *Negotiations and Change* (Thomas Kochan and David Lipsky, eds., Cornell University Press), John-Paul McDuffie argues that work organization in both North America and Europe has moved in the direction of the team-based model found in the Japanese lean production system, but that the pace of reform varies from plant to plant. According to McDuffie, the lean production system was introduced to and spread among European automakers in the early 1980s, much earlier than in the US auto industry. The reasons American automakers were slower in adopting lean production are that (a) flexibility in the production system was less important as there was less variety among car models; (b) there was less pressure to change work organization because market conditions were good; and (c) the UAW strongly resisted work organization change. Factors that spurred earlier adoption of lean production and teams by European automakers included an increasing variety of models, which required flexible production, and the fact that Japanese automakers were far more competitive internationally than their European counterparts. While the US auto industry was slower than the European auto industry in introducing lean production, both moved toward lean production and the team approach, not because of team "autonomy" but in order to survive in the intensely competitive international auto market.[8]

According to McDuffie, Japanese workers themselves do not think of their work style as being "team-based," as many US researchers have asserted. To researchers familiar with the strict job demarcation that has traditionally characterized the US auto industry, it may look as though Japanese workers are helping each other, but in fact they are only endeavoring to improve productivity and quality. With their wages determined partly by merit, Japanese workers strive to earn higher wages by making contributions to productivity and quality gains. Misunderstanding this, US researchers exaggerated the idea of "teamwork." From the 1990s, US researchers gradually developed a more accurate and nuanced understanding of Japanese work organization, for which the phrase "team-based work" is misleading. McDuffie's work in 2003 was a significant step toward understanding that the driving force behind work organization in the Japanese model is relentless pursuit of improved productivity and quality, and that focusing excessively on the "team concept" misses the point. The essential character of Japanese work organization is not captured by keywords such as "team concept" alone. Rather, it lies in the details of performance management and its relationship to specific elements of the work system. Teamwork does play a role in this, and McDuffie continues to use the keyword "teamwork," but he does not argue that teams are "autonomous."

How teams actually function

For understanding the relationship between teamwork and the improvement of productivity and quality, the research of Pil and McDuffie (1999), who studied and compared teams in Japanese auto plants, overseas plants of Japanese automakers, and Big Three plants in the United States, is useful.[9] These researchers found that teams were used in all the plants of Japanese automakers, both domestic and overseas, but in only a third of Big Three plants. About half of all Big Three workers belonged to a team, whereas at

Japanese domestic and overseas plants all workers are in teams. Aspects of work that were affected by teams included: (1) the use of new technology, (2) assignment of workers to work solely on the production line, (3) review of work methods, (4) evaluation of results, (5) responding to complaints/ dissatisfactions, (6) the pace of work, and (7) the amount of work done in one day. The influence of teams on work was strongest in Japanese plants, next-strongest in overseas plants of Japanese automakers, and weakest in Big Three plants.

Team leaders were sometimes elected by team members in US plants, while in Japan management generally appoints team leaders. Regarding problem-solving activities, the percentage of workers that participated in quality circles was 80% in Japanese auto plants, 27% in Japanese automakers' overseas plants, and 26% in Big Three US plants. The average number of suggestions or proposals per employee per year was 23.2 in Japanese plants, 3.9 in Japanese automakers' overseas plants, and 0.26 in Big Three US plants. The proportion of suggestions or proposals actually implemented was 84% in Japanese plants, 70% in Japanese automakers' overseas plants, and 41% in Big Three US plants. As these numbers show, teams play a more active role, and are more management-driven, in Japanese auto plants than in US auto plants.

While the above differences in team activities were found among Japanese plants, Japanese automakers' overseas plants, and Big Three US plants, surveys did not reveal significant differences among the three in productivity. Regarding quality, a JD Power and Associates survey showed no statistical difference between Japanese automakers' domestic and overseas plants, but found that quality was lower in Big Three US plants.

A case study of Saturn

In *Learning from Saturn: Possibilities for Corporate Governance and Employee Relations* (2001) Saul A. Rubinstein and Thomas A. Kochan present the results of their research on Saturn, the wholly owned subsidiary of GM that was launched with a newly built auto manufacturing plant in Tennessee, an innovative labor agreement, and workplace practices that were unconventional by US standards. It is well known that GM learned much from NUMMI, its joint venture with Toyota, and that it incorporated some of the work practices used at NUMMI in its own plants. However, according to Rubinstein and Kochan, GM's introduction of the lean production system not only took employees' interests into account but also considered the interests of shareholders. So, GM's version of lean production had its own particular characteristics and did not always match the Toyota way.[10]

At Saturn, GM's intention was to build a plant and production system that was not constrained by traditional job control unionism, and that would produce autos with high productivity and the quality required to be competitive with foreign automakers. In this regard, the Saturn example gives us many facts to explore. Rubinstein and Kochan describe four elements of work organization at the Saturn plant: (1) self-directed work teams, (2) problem-solving teams, (3) labor–management committees, and (4) partnering of operating and management staff on the production line. However, their description of these elements of work organization, and their neglect of other specific and concrete factors of the production process, result in a superficial analysis that overlooks many things that affect productivity and quality. While their study is valuable, it is in some ways reminiscent of the naïve belief of 1980s researchers that introducing the team concept would naturally and automatically lead to productivity and quality improvements.

Generally speaking, when the operators of a manufacturing plant aim to improve productivity and quality, we try to understand their efforts and plans through field research at the shop floor level. For example, in the Taylorism approach, production management was mainly decided by the industrial engineer and the foreman. The union fought against change in work organization by writing grievances. To write a revealing study of a case of work organization reform, it is necessary to describe many facts in detail, such as the allocation of workers, production standards, workers' workloads, line speed, and how work reorganization affects workers. Management efforts to persuade workers to accept change and negotiations between management and the union also need to be described in detail, as well as productivity and quality indices, how targets are set, management plans for attaining targets, meetings between worker representatives and management, and the makeup and functions of production worker teams. Unless all of this is presented accurately and in-depth, the reality of a change in work organization cannot be understood. We believe that past research in the United States has not illuminated the issues noted above in sufficient depth.

How many elements of performance management did Rubinstein and Kochan's research of Saturn make clear? According to the authors, workers and the union at Saturn were more actively involved in management control and governance than at other plants. Table 1.1 shows Rubinstein and Kochan's framework for analyzing the four main features that made Saturn different from other US auto plants.[11]

Let us discuss and analyze these features one by one starting with *self-directed work teams*, which are called "work units" at Saturn. While the "spirit" of autonomy is a strong part of the team concept at Saturn, the

Table 1.1 Framework for analyzing the union's roles in governance and management at GM Saturn

Union leadership	Union membership
Off-line ③ Labor–management committees (Decision rings)	② Problem-solving teams (Problem resolution circles)
On-line ④ Partnering of operating and middle management staff	① Self-directed work teams (Work units)

Source: Rubinstein and Kochan, *Learning from Saturn*, p. 26.

actual teams are not completely autonomous; in order to make teams effective, representatives of management, such as foremen, team leaders, or module advisors play a decisive role.[12] The reason for this is that under traditional job control unionism, workers performed their jobs in accordance with prescribed rules contained in the labor agreement. Under the team concept, workers have more discretion and decisions are more decentralized, but given the historical background of workers following instructions rather than making decisions themselves, it was inevitable that management would exert a strong influence on teams and how they operate.

The autonomous nature of teams was emphasized in many studies of the team concept in the US auto industry. But at Saturn, because the activities and goals of teams in the workplace were more advanced, a greater level of management direction and control was required. American researchers discovered this, but their descriptions lack the detail necessary to understand how this work organization functioned. For example, Rubinstein and Kochan explain that both the autonomous spirit of the team and administrative oversight were important, but they do not clarify the specific authority allocation relationship between teams and management. Labor history textbooks describe how industrial engineers (IEs) and supervisors unilaterally decided the allocation of the assembly line workers and assigned workloads in traditional American production sites. Workers are required to work according to a specified job description, and if they do not comply they are subject to discipline by management. If a worker objects to an assignment or change, he or she can use the grievance procedure. This was a static system in the sense that production activities were performed exactly as per the rule. In other words, in the past, there was no place for autonomy on the part of line workers; they just had to follow the manual. If, at Saturn, workers were given a measure of autonomy, what did that autonomy entail? What activities and decisions, in what areas, did workers carry out on their own, and what things were decided or guided by IEs, team leaders, foremen, or module advisors? (Module advisor was a newly created position for union members at the workplace level which enabled decisions to be made jointly by labor and management in a spirit of partnership.) And how did the workers and management representatives communicate and work together? These "details" are critical and need to be clarified. Simply saying, as Rubinstein and Kochan do in their book, that "Autonomy is being pursued as a philosophy" is insufficient for helping us to understand the direct relationship between autonomy and the improvement of quality and productivity.

Problem-solving teams, the second feature of Saturn that distinguishes it from other US auto plants, refers to groups of union members that work "off-line," i.e., apart from the production line, to solve problems. According to Rubinstein and Kochan, these are important entities that are given authority, resources, and work beyond the scope of self-directed work teams. Especially important at Honda and Toyota, problem-solving teams spend months or a year focusing on issues such as safety, reducing costs, or quality assurance. Supervisors are required to make concrete proposals to address these issues. Saturn also had problem-solving groups that worked "off-line," but they were less important than at Honda and Toyota; at Saturn, "on-line" teams played a bigger role in problem-solving.

In Japan, *kaizen* (literally, "improvement") teams, composed of workers, which focus on reducing costs, improving quality, and improving the capacity utilization rate, roughly correspond to problem-solving teams at Saturn. Rubinstein and Kochan do not present much detailed information about Saturn's problem-solving teams, such as the number of workers on a team, the level of authority a team has, the division of labor within a team, and who is eligible to be a member of a team. But their recognition of the importance of "problem-solving" and "continuous improvement activities" in achieving advances in productivity and quality control represents a major advance in research in the United States, which had previously missed this point because it was overly focused on the "team concept" and the fact of workers working together.

The third feature is *labor–management committees*. These present a new topic for research on American labor relations and work organization reform. Conventionally, in the American automobile factory, it was rare for the management side to consult in advance with the union side regarding management rights and decisions. Joint labor–management committees were therefore ground-breaking, but also difficult to implement, given the historical background and prevailing attitudes.

Joint labor–management committees at Saturn were deployed at multiple levels. At the company level was the Strategic Action Council. At the plant level was the Manufacturing Action Council. There were also labor–management teams at the business unit, module, and work unit levels.[13] Initially, decision-making was decentralized to the committees at each level, information was shared between labor and management, and the union was given the opportunity to provide input affecting production decisions. This was possible because, unlike other GM plants, Saturn did not have to abide by the National Labor Relations Agreement. It could therefore develop its own special style of governance, including an institutionalized labor–management consultation system. During the 1990s, however, the view gradually grew within GM that Saturn should not be treated differently from other GM divisions, and decision-making became more centralized, shifting to GM corporate headquarters. As a result, the Manufacturing Action Council's control over improvement activities and organizational learning at the Saturn plant diminished. By 1999 the Manufacturing Action Council had lost much of its meaning, and its weekly meetings were reduced to being held only every other week.

Decentralization of decision-making at Saturn was also hindered by differences among the plant's body, powertrain, and assembly departments in their support for labor–management collaboration. Another problem was that the retention of managers at Saturn was low: the average tenure was only one year as, according to Rubinstein and Kochan, managers were more interested in advancing their personal careers, which required giving attention to GM headquarters, than in developing their departments at Saturn over time.

While the attempt to improve labor relations through the introduction of labor–management committees at Saturn was ground-breaking, Rubinstein and Kochan blame the management side rather than workers and the union for the lack of success of this effort. Their book also describes other situations where labor–management cooperation proved difficult. However, they provide little detail about factors that would better illuminate why labor–management committees struggled to function successfully, such as the authority relations and decision-making processes between different levels of management.

The fourth feature, *partnering of operating and middle management staff*, was a new form of labor–management cooperation on the production line, with members from the union side and management side participating equally, in a one-to-one ratio. Originating in 1988, the initial group was made up of 100 appointed members: 50 from the union side plus 50 from the management side. One of their objectives was to incorporate the voice of union members into day-to-day management of the assembly line. This made Saturn unique, as union members were not involved to this degree in the decision-making process at other GM plants. Labor and management jointly selected the module advisors.

Like the joint labor–management committees described above, this partnering arrangement was formally adopted by both labor and management.

Rubinstein and Kochan write that through this system the union and management were able to exchange opinions in daily conversations concerning production methods, production volume, and other issues. However, details about how the system actually operated are unclear, including, for example, how module advisors, the foreman, and team leaders were involved in the partnering. Saturn was the only production site where this labor relations structure was implemented.[14]

Overall, we can understand from Rubinstein and Kochan that new forms of labor–management cooperation were attempted at Saturn, as described above. However, many details of those efforts remain unexplained.

Issues that need to be clarified

What is lacking in Rubinstein and Kochan's study of Saturn? In short, we believe it is a concrete, detailed, and systematic investigation.

Unlike at traditional GM auto plants, Saturn was not constrained by conventional job control unionism. Management aimed to improve productivity and quality through the four forms of work organization described above. But the direct relationship between these and the improvement of productivity and quality is not explored or explained in sufficient depth. For example, their book leaves the following questions unanswered.

- How did semi-autonomous teams contribute to reducing man-hours?
- What were the obstacles that teams encountered?
- How did the team concept contribute to improving the direct run rate (the non-defective production yield) and lowering the defective product rate and the frequency of production line stops?
- What were the limits of management authority under GM's team concept?
- What did the overall management system look like, and who was responsible for it?
- How often were meetings held with Saturn management to make plans to achieve targets sent down from GM corporate headquarters?
- What was the structure of committees or units responsible for quality and productivity management, and kind of conflict that occurred there?
- What kind of conflict occurred when standardized work tasks were changed because of a model change or a change in line speed?
- Who was responsible for making decisions and getting consensus from affected workers?
- What role did the module advisor play in the process of improving productivity and quality?

- What was the role of Saturn's problem-solving groups in improving productivity and quality?
- How were the labor–management committees positioned in the organization?
- What is the relationship among the four entities shown in Table 1.1?

These are among the many things that should be explored more deeply. There are a huge number of tasks in an auto plant that must be developed and carried out according to plan. Whether a plant can be organized successfully depends on the actual people working on the shop floor labor. Even though GM closely studied the Toyota production method through NUMMI, there remains a gap in work organization between GM and Toyota.

In the systematic planning of all the parts and all the steps that go into the assembly of an automobile, specific labor tasks need to be clarified in detail. This means that labor should be positioned at the center of management activities. Performance management and planning, and activities designed to improve productivity and quality, can never be discussed separately from the performance management system. Unfortunately, Rubinstein and Kochan do not connect labor with the performance management system. This issue needs to be addressed in research on American work organization reform.

Knowledge-driven work and "kaizen" activities

Knowledge-driven work: Points previously discussed

The 2015 book *Inside the Ford–UAW Transformation*, by Joel Cutcher-Gershenfeld, Dan Brooks, and Martin Mulloy, contains the most recent empirical research on changes in the labor–management relationship between the UAW and Ford. This book focuses on historical "pivotal events" to analyze the current situation of the US auto industry. In Chapter 5, the authors argue that the post-industrial global economy is characterized by an increase in knowledge-driven work, and that a broad range of jobs are becoming ever more "knowledge-driven." They analyze the history of organizational change at Ford plants by focusing on the following "pivotal events":

1) Ford Total Productive Maintenance Roots, 1982
2) Mazda Flat Rock, 1987
3) Romeo Engine Plant, 1988
4) Continuous Improvement and FPS (Ford Production System) Rollout, 1996–1999

5) Team Start and Stop Designations, 1999
6) UAW Glass Plants, 2002
7) Hourly Six Sigma Black Belts, 2003–2008
8) Powertrain Plant of the Future, 2007–2008
9) Team-Based Agreements, 2011

This book is not the first in which the notion of "knowledge-driven" work appears. In 1998, Cutcher-Gershenfeld and his colleagues introduced this keyword for the first time in their book *Knowledge-Driven Work: Unexpected Lessons from Japanese and United States Work Practices*. In this work they wrote that Japanese economic power had weakened since the 1980s, but that managers and scholars in the United States and Europe still had many things to learn from Japanese-style management and work organization. They argued that in the coming "knowledge economy," "intangible" knowledge as well as "tangible" knowledge would play a pivotal role in Japanese auto plants, and that "knowledge-driven work" would also become more important in US auto plant work organization. In their 2015 work, the authors continued to focus on "knowledge-driven work," applying the concept to work organization at Ford. They also focus on "continuous improvement," or "kaizen" as it is called in Japanese. Kaizen is a critical concept in discussion of work organization change in the US auto industry, and an important element of our research.

Knowledge-driven work: Points that need further discussion

"Knowledge-driven work" and "continuous improvement"

Cutcher-Gershenfeld et al. provide a general description of "continuous improvement" and how it is organized, but they do not analyze the relationship between "knowledge-driven work" and "continuous improvement" in detail, nor do they show how these fit into the overall production system. What is missing is elucidation of the specific mechanisms by which "continuous improvement" leads to improved quality and productivity, including detailed examples, goals, and problems encountered in implementing "continuous improvement."

To start with, when we consider "continuous improvement," a distinction should be made between "routine work" (repetitive or usual) "non-routine work" (non-repetitive or unusual). In Japan, kaizen is strongly related to the non-routine work of direct production workers. In the present book, we describe in detail the mechanisms and relationships between "continuous improvement" and improving quality and productivity.

Non-routine work

Next, we focus on "non-routine work" by direct production workers in an auto plant. Non-routine work is where kaizen is applied in the Japanese auto industry, with production workers motivated by a strong incentive system.[15] The aim of kaizen is to improve quality and reduce costs. Needless to say, there are many ways to do this. In Japan, production workers, as non-routine work, work on improving quality and reducing costs by (1) improving machine up-time, (2) reducing the defect rate, and (3) reducing man-hours. By contrast, in the traditional production system in US auto plants, industrial engineers and supervisors were solely responsible for these. Improving machine up-time, reducing the rate of defects, and reducing man-hours are important goals of recent work organization changes in the US auto industry, but Cutcher-Gershenfeld et al. do not focus deeply enough on these.

Remuneration for routine work is carried out under the concept of "equal pay for equal work." Remuneration for non-routine work, on the other hand, is carried out through a merit pay scheme in Japan. This is because many different kinds of workers, of different pay grades, participate in non-routine work; merit pay allows an individual to be rewarded appropriately for non-routine work regardless of his or her pay level for routine work. In addition, through this merit pay system, excellent workers can be promoted to higher-level, non-union managerial positions. There are cases in the Japanese auto industry of production line workers being promoted to positions as high as member of the board of directors, or even vice president. At the same time, there are other workers who remain production line workers until they reach retirement age, which is usually 60.

(1) IMPROVING MACHINE UP-TIME

In the general assembly department, the production line often stops, creating down-time. In order to improve productivity, plant managers strive to increase machine up-time. This means eliminating or reducing both long periods and short periods of down-time. As Koike and Inoki (1987) have pointed out, even short periods of down-time have a negative effect on plant productivity, and production workers' knowledge and ideas can be used to reduce these.[16] This is because not only quality specialists but also general production workers can identify minor irregularities or defects on the line and point them out, allowing them to be dealt with as soon as possible. As we will describe later in this book, US auto plants are gradually trying to use production workers' skills and knowledge to reduce down-time in this way.

(2) REDUCING THE DEFECT RATE

"Direct run rate" (DRR) is the ratio of vehicles built with no known defects after final inspection as a percentage of the total number of vehicles built on a production shift. Generally speaking, the products that come off a manufacturer's production line include some defective products that cannot be sold in the market unless they receive additional work to fix the defects. So manufacturers continually work to lower the percentage of defective products and increase the percentage of products with acceptable quality. Detroit's Big Three have been making efforts to improve the direct run rate through their work organization reform, but there are few empirical studies that have explored the relationship between work organization change and the direct run rate. Analysis of data concerning this important metric is needed.

(3) REDUCING MAN-HOURS

Man-hour is a unit of measurement based on the amount of work performed by an average worker in one hour. Reorganizing the workload or manufacturing process to reduce man-hours leads to a reduction in the number of workers needed and reduced labor costs. In the American auto industry, reducing man-hours is connected with lay-offs, and has historically created significant tensions between the UAW and the auto manufacturers. In the Japanese auto industry, on the other hand, workers made redundant due to man-hour reductions are generally not laid off, but shifted to other jobs or other plants. Excellent workers are often promoted from production line work to administrative positions. This is a major difference between Japan and the United States.

The UAW and continuous improvement

"Pay-for-performance," "pay-for-skill," and "pay-for-knowledge" are forms of merit pay. Meritocracy for blue-collar workers, which took root in Japan following the Second World War, is highly valued by Japanese production workers as it gives them opportunities for higher pay and advancement that they did not have in prewar Japan.

Without a merit pay system for UAW workers, is it realistic to expect production workers in the United States to engage in non-routine work aimed at improving machine up-time, reducing the defect rate, and reducing man-hours? How feasible is continuous improvement by production workers without the motivation of monetary rewards? This is a critical question that most researchers, including Cutcher-Gershenfeld et al., do not address. In Chapter 2 of this book, we trace the historical evolution of job control unionism, especially the UAW's seniority rule, using past arbitration records concerning seniority disputes.

Continuous improvement in Japan

When most researchers in the United States discuss employment relations in Japan, they tend to focus on elements such as the seniority system, "lifetime employment," teamwork, and commitment. Merit pay for union members has received little attention, despite the fact it supports the kaizen system.

As the following chapters of this book will show, all of the features of work organization reform, including knowledge-driven work and continuous improvement, can be grasped comprehensively and systematically in the framework of the performance management system. At GM in recent years, great emphasis has been placed on GMS as a strong performance management framework. But the overall picture of how GMS was developed, the way it operates, and the challenges it presents have not yet been written about in sufficient detail. This is why in this book we investigate, analyze, and describe the relationship between employment relations and the performance management system in great depth.

Conclusion

The following summarizes the main points that have been discussed in this chapter.

Discussion of work organization reform increased in the United States during the 1980s, with the "team concept," a feature of the Japanese workplace, attracting considerable attention. The basic idea as understood by many researchers was that if workers have the chance to work cooperatively in autonomous teams, increased job satisfaction and autonomy will lead to improved productivity and quality. We consider this view to be superficial and naïve.

In the 1990s, the term "diversification" was used to describe the state and direction of work organization reform in the United States. Job descriptions in the Japanese workplace are more loosely defined than in the traditional American workplace. The degree of autonomy of workers and teams in Japan, however, is not necessarily high, being subject to a strict management control system. These facts have gradually come to be recognized and discussed by researchers in the United States.

While some US studies note that Japanese work organizations are under strong management control, no scholars have researched the management control systems of Japanese companies in detail, including the direct relationship between the shop floor and management. The most important plant performance indicators for management are the productivity and quality improvement indexes. There is a need for in-depth investigation of the details of plant management control systems and employment relations.

Rubinstein and Kochan introduce four forms of work organization at Saturn designed to improve productivity and quality: self-directed work teams, problem-solving teams, joint labor–management committees, and partnering of operating and middle management staff. However, their description lacks detail and does not show how these are explicitly linked to performance management.

Cutcher-Gershenfeld et al. point out the importance of "continuous improvement" activities and knowledge-driven work, but they deal with these separately, neglecting to explore and explain the relationship between them and how they are regulated by the performance management system. This makes it difficult to understand the direction of work organization reform in the United States.

In conclusion, previous studies in the United States are inadequate for understanding performance management in Japanese and US auto plants. In the following chapters of this book, we present the results of extensive field research in order to fill the void left by previous academic studies.

Notes

1 Shinohara (2003), chap. 1.
2 Ishida (2003), chap. 3.
3 Shinohara (2003), chap. 1.
4 After the 1980s, many employment relations researchers believed that the workplace and labor–management system that had come out of the New Deal era had been dismantled; consequently, academic interest in actual work conditions gradually decreased.
5 Katz and Darbishire (2000), p. 10.
6 *Ibid.*, p. 41.
7 Adler, Kochan, MacDuffie, Pil and Rubinstein (1997), p. 83.
8 MacDuffie (2003), pp. 106–107.
9 Pil and MacDuffie (1999), Chap. 2.
10 Rubinstein and Kochan (2001), p. 139.
11 *Ibid.*, pp. 26–54.
12 *Ibid.*, pp. 45–48, 129, 141.
13 *Ibid.*, p. 50.
14 *Ibid.*, p. 54.
15 Ishida et al. (1997).
16 Koike and Inoki (1987).

References

Adler, Paul, T. A. Kochan, J. P. MacDuffie, F. K. Pil, & S. A. Rubinstein. (1997). "United States: Variations on a Theme." In Thomas A. Kochan, Russell D. Lansbury, & John Paul MacDuffie (Eds) *After Lean Production: Evolving Employment Practices in the World Economy*. Ithaca: Cornell University Press.

Cutcher-Gershenfeld, Joel. (1998). *Knowledge Driven Work*. New York: Oxford University Press.

Cutcher-Gershenfeld, Joel, Dan Brooks, & Martin Mulloy. (2015). *Inside the Ford-UAW Transformation*. Boston: The MIT Press.

Ishida, Mitsuo. (2003). *Shigoto No Shakai Kagaku (in Japanese, "The Social Science of Work: The Frontier of Labor Research")*. Kyoto: Minerva Shobo.

Ishida, Mitsuo, Norio Hisamoto, Hiroyuki Fujimura, & Fumito Matsumura. (1997). *Nihon No Riin Seisan Houshiki (in Japanese, "Lean Production System in Japan")*. Tokyo: Chuo Keizaisha.

Katz, Harry C., & O. Darbishire. (2000). *Converging Divergences*. Ithaca: Cornel University Press.

Koike, Kazuo, & Takenori Inoki. (1987). *Jinzai Keisei No Kokusai hikaku*. Tokyo: Toyo Keizai Shinpo-sha.

MacDuffie, John Paul. (2003). "Leaning Toward Teams." In Thomas A. Kochan & David B. Lipsky (Eds) *Negotiations and Change*. Ithaca: Cornell University Press.

Pil, Frits K., & J. P. MacDuffie. (1999). "Transferring Competitive Advantage Across Borders: A Study of Japanese Transplants in North America." In Jeffrey Liker, M. Fruin, & P. Adler (Eds) *Remade in America*. New York: Oxford University Press.

Rubinstein, Saul A., & T. A. Kochan. (2001). *Learning from Saturn: A Look at the Boldest Experiment in Corporate Governance and Employee Relations*. Ithaca: Cornell University Press.

Shinohara, Kenichi. (2003). *Tenkanki No Amerika Roushi Kaikei (in Japanese, "American Labor Relations in Transition: Work Organizational Reform in the Automobile Industry")*. Kyoto: Minerva Shobo.

Womack, James, D. Jones, & D. Roos. (1990). *The Machine That Changed the World*. New York: Free Press.

2 The development of seniority rights and establishment of rules for job transfer and promotion in the United States

General Motors Corporation

Introduction

This chapter has two main goals. The first is to lay out in detail the historical development of job transfer and promotion rules and the place of seniority in unionized American firms. Understanding these key elements of traditional work organization is essential for understanding subsequent work organization reform in the United States. The second goal is to describe arbitration awards and to highlight their connection to collective bargaining agreements and their influence on the evolution of transfer and promotion rules and the seniority system. The chapter focuses on General Motors and the GM National Agreement, but as there are only minor differences between the GM Agreement and those of the other American automakers, what is described here is representative of the overall US auto industry.

Kazuo Koike has written that work organization in the United States is based on "obvious rules," that is, rules with no room for misunderstanding.[1] It is true that, at first glance, the language of the national auto agreements is relatively simple and seems quite clear and easy to understand. This is partly due to the fact that the National Agreements prescribe broad, basic rules concerning work organization. Behind the contract language, however, lie many historical conflicts between labor and management which remain hidden from readers. A single word can have a deep meaning that cannot be appreciated unless one has an intimate familiarity with the history and the reality of the actual production system inside the factory. In this sense, American collective bargaining agreements are, in fact, very difficult to understand.

The process leading up to today's collective bargaining agreements and related issues has not been well documented. For this reason, many studies have appeared on work organization reform that pay little attention to the historical development of transfer, promotion, and seniority rules. Yet, work organization reform taken up in the United States since the 1980s—including, for example, the introduction of the team concept, flexibility, and commitment—cannot be

DOI: 10.4324/9781003282426-2

fully understood in the absence of a detailed examination of the historical labor contracts and past arbitration records that regulate traditional work organization. This chapter therefore clarifies the role that both national and local agreements have played in seniority-related issues as they impact the implementation and governance of the GMS at GM factories in the United States.

One of the characteristics of traditional work organization in the American automobile industry is the strong degree to which it is regulated by the United Automobile Workers union (UAW). Work rules, wages, and other aspects of work organization are stipulated by collective bargaining agreements, which in the American auto industry are subject to negotiations every four years. Collective bargaining agreements are broadly divided into the National Agreement, which covers almost all GM factories in the United States, and local agreements that cover each individual factory and address their unique circumstances on a different set of bargaining subjects. Two salient features of the American workplace that influence and have been influenced by collective bargaining agreements are the so-called "equal pay for equal work" rule and the large number of different job classifications; these are closely related to each other and to seniority and are important determinants in job transfer and promotion decisions.

Arbitration awards are an important mechanism for settling labor disputes in the United States and have exerted a strong influence on contract language in subsequent collective bargaining agreements. Historically, a large number of grievances were written by the union on behalf of the workers they represent. Most of these grievances are settled at the workplace level between the local union and management. But some are appealed to higher bodies and, if they remain unresolved, ultimately presented before a neutral third-party arbitrator, whose ruling is binding on both parties. The resulting arbitration awards have sometimes led to significant changes in workplace rules and practices and altered labor–management relations.

By elucidating the historical development of job transfer and promotion rules and the place of seniority in the US auto industry and the role played by arbitration awards in shaping collective bargaining agreements, this chapter sets the stage for consideration of the reform of GM factories that began in the 1980s under competitive pressures from Japanese automakers and which used Toyota systems as a model.

Development of job transfer and promotion rules

Early development of the seniority system

Before considering worker transfer and promotion practices, it is necessary to understand the history of seniority rights. The development of the seniority system is closely related to the role of the foreman or field supervisor at the factory. In the earliest form of "scientific management"—sometimes called Taylorism, after its pioneer Frederick Taylor—the foreman held a great deal of power, not only in monitoring and supervising the work process but in making employee transfer, promotion, and layoff decisions. For this reason, creating a seniority system necessarily meant decreasing the authority of the foremen.[2]

Originally, seniority did not play a role in the transfer and promotion of employees in the US automobile industry. According to Gersuny (1982), the idea of seniority rights first appeared in the United States in the 1890s,[3] but it did not become a workplace rule at that time. It was perceived by some as a "mad theory of some namby-pamby socialist."[4] In the early 1920s, seniority rules began to be discussed during collective bargaining in some manufacturing industries.[5] However, it was only with the establishment of the National Labor Relations Act in 1935, and in response to demands from many labor unions for secure employment rather than wage increases, that the stage was set for the seniority system to flourish. Among rank and file union members, the seniority system became popular as a means to protect jobs and bring order to the workplace. Decisions about who would be laid off first during a workforce reduction and when they would be recalled to work were all made according to seniority rules established in the collective bargaining agreement. It is said that in companies with labor unions, the proportion of collective bargaining agreements that included layoff clauses nearly doubled between the 1920s and 1930s.[6] And in non-union companies, starting around 1935, the adoption of seniority rules began to be used as a defensive measure to prevent unionization. Personnel departments in non-union companies were also motivated to expand seniority rights in order to increase their authority vis-à-vis foremen with whom they were in conflict.[7]

The expansion of the seniority system did not proceed smoothly, however. While seniority rights were originally established as a means of strengthening employment security, labor unions began to demand their extension to job transfers and employee promotion. Management adopted a cautious attitude toward linking seniority with promotion, fearing that promotion according to seniority rather than ability would negatively affect factory efficiency.[8] Foremen also opposed expanding seniority rights to job transfers and employee promotion, as it diminished their power to choose which workers would fill openings in their area. In the past, foremen had total responsibility for and authority over the job assignments of subordinate workers. But as a result of the expansion of the seniority system, the union and the personnel department now directly negotiated how job assignments would be made. This reduced the power of foremen. Despite the resistance of management and foremen, and similar conflict over layoffs, the seniority system gradually spread through the automobile industry during the latter half of the 1930s, and by the 1940s employee transfers, promotion, and layoffs were firmly tied to seniority. The National Agreement drafted in March 1937 stated, with regard to transfer and promotion, "The transferring of employees is solely the responsibility of Management."[9] At this time layoffs and recall were not covered, but gradually seniority rights came to include job transfers, shift preference, layoffs, and recall; 35% of the contents of the 1937 agreement related to seniority rights.[10]

Phase 1: The June 24, 1940, revision of the agreement

Throughout the latter half of the 1930s, the UAW pushed for the adoption of seniority rights. In the 1940 collective bargaining agreement between the UAW and GM, the contract language defining seniority rights included the transfer of workers to open jobs for the first time. Specifically, the following sentences were added:

> Placed no restrictions on management's right to transfer except that in transferring employee seniority will be secondary to other qualifications but will be given reasonable consideration. Recognized that claims of discrimination for union activity in connection with transfer could be taken up as grievances.[11]

In this way, although seniority rights were taken into consideration for the first time, their role was only secondary. This fell short of meeting the union's demands. From the standpoint of the UAW, the sentence "seniority will be secondary to other qualifications but will be given reasonable consideration" was unsatisfactory.

On November 28, three months after the effective date of the 1940 agreement, a grievance concerning seniority rights and employee transfer was filed by the union on behalf of paint department worker G. Paint carrier N was chosen by management for an open job in the glazed spray booth. N had prior experience in glazed spraying, but G had more seniority than N. The union argued that management's decision to give the open job to N, despite G having more seniority, was discrimination against G due to his union activities.

This grievance was ultimately argued before an arbitrator, and the decision was handed down on April 11, 1941.[12] The arbitrator dismissed the grievance, ruling that employee transfer to open jobs was based on a practice that had been followed for 37 years and which gave management the exclusive right to make job assignment decisions. In the opinion of the arbitrator, there was no discrimination against G due to his being a union member. The assignment of N to the open position was judged to be appropriate because N had been a glaze sprayer before he was a paint carrier, and his assignment to the paint department was temporary; he was promised that he would later be returned to the glazed spray booth.

Thus, in the end, employee seniority did not play a role in the filling of the job opening. The arbitration decision was made based on the 1940 National Agreement. The intention of the phrase "seniority will be secondary to other qualifications but will be given reasonable consideration" was ambiguous. In other words, the problem for the union was the collective bargaining agreement itself; it did not make clear the weight that would be given to seniority in employee transfer decisions. Because the contract language was vague, the arbitration decision could not be criticized.

Table 2.1 shows the changes that were made to Paragraph 63, which covers transfers and promotion, in the 16 National Agreements from 1940 to 1979, and related arbitration cases and awards. In addition to the arbitration cases listed in Table 2.1, there are 12 arbitration awards relating to job transfer and seniority based on Paragraph 8 of the 1940 agreement covering the transfer of employees.[13] Only two of these were decided in favor of the union. As explained above, the 1940 agreement was not satisfactory from the union's point of view with regard to job transfer.[14] Therefore, in the negotiations on revising the agreement in 1941, the union insisted that employee job transfers should be decided strictly on the basis of seniority, with the most senior employee given priority.

Phase 2: The June 3, 1941, revision of the agreement

In the National Agreement drafted in 1940, regulations that governed the use of seniority in employee transfer decisions were, for the union side, ambiguous and insufficient. Therefore, in the negotiations of the 1941 agreement, the union demanded that seniority be made a stronger determinant in the movement of employees. Management resisted this demand in an effort to maintain their ability to assign workers to jobs with as little input from the union as possible.

As a result of the union demands, the following contract language was agreed to in the new agreement[15]:

> The transferring of employees is the sole responsibility of management, subject to following: In the advancement of employees to higher paid jobs when ability, merit and capacity are equal, employees with the longest seniority will be given preference.

Table 2.1 Changes made to Article 63 in the 16 National Agreements (1940 to 1979) and related arbitration cases and awards

	Changes to Paragraph 63 of the National Agreement	Number of arbitration awards relating to Paragraph 63	Number of cases won by UAW in arbitration awards	Number of cases UAW won/number of arbitration awards with promotion being the main issue of contention	Number of cases UAW won/number of arbitration awards with job transfer being the main issue of contention
1940 Agreement	Seniority made a secondary consideration	12	2	1/9	1/3
1941 Agreement	When ability, merit, and capability are equal, employee with the longest seniority will be given preference	21	6	5/12	1/9
1942 Agreement	No change	33	7	5/26	2/7
1945 Agreement	Distinction made between temporary and permanent job transfers	2	0	0/2	0/0
1946 Agreement	Paragraph 63 split into paragraphs (a) and (b), covering promotion and transfer, respectively	24	4	3/14	1/10
1948 Agreement	No change	8	3	2/7	1/1
1950 Agreement	Special note added for cases where department is small	15	6	5/13	1/2
1955 Agreement	Prior transfer provision rights strengthened	5	0	0/5	0/0
1958 Agreement	No change	1	1	1/1	0/0
1961 Agreement	No change	0	0	0/0	0/0
1964 Agreement	Additional statements added regarding promotion and pay	1	0	0/1	0/0
1967 Agreement	No change	2	0	0/2	0/0
1970 Agreement	Descriptive changes regarding promotion	1	1	1/1	0/0
1973 Agreement	No change	1	0	0/1	0/0

(Continued)

Table 2.1 (Continued)

Changes to Paragraph 63 of the National Agreement	Number of arbitration awards relating to Paragraph 63	Number of cases won by UAW in arbitration awards	Number of cases UAW won/number of arbitration awards with promotion being the main issue of contention	Number of cases UAW won/number of arbitration awards with job transfer being the main issue of contention
1976 Agreement Distinction made between intra-departmental and extra-departmental promotion rules	0	0	0/0	0/0
1979 Agreement Minor modifications based on 1976 Agreement	0	0	0/0	0/0
Total numbers	126	29	23/94	6/32

Source: Past arbitration awards (UAW-GM Umpire Decisions) are from GM Department, UAW Headquarters, and past National Agreements are from Walter Reuther Library, Wayne State University.

Notes:
1. Author's aggregation of arbitration awards for job transfers and promotions.
2. In the 1940 Agreement, the transfer and promotion clause is classified as Paragraph 8, not Paragraph 63.
3. The number of UAW victories shown includes partial victories.

This significantly increased the weight of seniority rights, from "secondary but given reasonable consideration" to the role of a "tiebreaker" when the abilities of candidates for promotion were the same.

This strengthening of seniority rights provisions satisfied the union although, predictably, it led to controversy over how to judge the "ability" of workers who sought open jobs in subsequent arbitration cases. New criteria established in the arbitration ruling issued at Chevrolet Gear & Axle on December 30, 1941, clarified the standard for evaluating competence.[16] The grievance that led to this ruling was filed on August 15, 1941. Employee T had been chosen rather than Employee M when a reliefman position became vacant.[17] M and T had similar abilities to perform the job, but M had more seniority, which led to the filing of the grievance. In the ruling the arbitrator argued that it was difficult to define the subjective factor of "ability," to wit:

1) It is impossible to accurately evaluate the relative abilities of individual employees.
2) Personal assessment by an on-site supervisor is accompanied by personal prejudice.
3) Seniority, however, is a clearly defined factor.
4) In order for multiple employees to be judged as having equal abilities, an appropriate process must be followed by management.[18]

With regard to that process, the arbitrator ruled that when deciding the promotion of an employee according to Paragraph 63, an employee's capability must be "outstanding," that is, "head and shoulders" above that of the other candidate(s), in order for the ability to take precedence over seniority.[19] Therefore, if management is unable to demonstrate a significant capability disparity, the promotion will be given to the candidate with the most seniority. In the case at hand, Employee T was not judged to be more skilled than Employee M; a skill disparity was not recognized and management's promotion of T was ruled invalid.

The same issue was argued before an arbitrator a few months later under the same principle that an "outstanding" and "head and shoulders" difference in ability was required in order for the ability to take priority over seniority in a promotion decision. In promotion cases at the GM Guide Lamp factory on January 12, 1942, and at Buick Motor on February 6 of the same year, the union prevailed.[20] In the past, the union had lost most transfer and promotion disputes taken to arbitration, but from the early 1940s onward, management had difficulty proving "outstanding" and "head and shoulders" ability differences. As a result, the number of factories in which promotion was almost entirely determined by seniority increased.

In this way, the basis for promotion changed from management discretion to the seniority of employees applying for a position. In the case of a non-promotion job transfer, however, seniority remained a non-factor, or a weak consideration at best. Therefore, during subsequent negotiations, the union focused on making seniority a determining factor in job transfer decisions. This effort did not result in new restrictions on transfer during negotiations in October of 1942. It finally came to fruition during negotiations in 1945.

Phase 3: The April 15, 1945, revision of the agreement

An examination of the historical development of transfer and promotion rules is incomplete without considering the role of the National War Labor Board (NWLB). In 1941, the United States entered World War II. If a strike were to occur in the middle of the war, production activity would stop as a matter of course. But strikes during WWII were contrary to American national policy, so in order to stabilize labor–management relations during the war, a "non-strike pledge" was signed by the unions in an agreement with management in 1941. In January 1942, the NWLB was established to handle labor disputes.

The NWLB was given the authority to settle workplace disputes based on the wartime authority of the US President.[21] When negotiations between labor and management were at an impasse, the US Conciliation Service, under the jurisdiction of the Department of Labor, would intervene, and if the impasse was not resolved, it would be handled by the NWLB.

In April 1945, during agreement amendment negotiations, the dispute over employee job transfers continued between the UAW and management. When labor–management negotiations failed to settle the question, the NWLB stepped in. The result was that new rules were added by the NWLB to the text governing employee transfer.

> The labor board announced that the "temporary" transfer of employees remained the "sole responsibility of Management," but that rules for "permanent transfers between occupational groups" must be negotiated locally and worked out in the local seniority agreement.[22]

Thus, intervention by the NWLB created a distinction between temporary and permanent transfer of employees; the contract language gave management the exclusive authority over temporary transfers, but not permanent transfers. "Temporary transfer" was defined as employee movement where the employee was scheduled to return to his/her former position within two months. Other than this, job transfer rules did not change significantly as a result of this revision of the agreement. Regarding the basis for permanent transfers, the NWLB decided to leave up to each individual factory. The distinction between temporary and permanent moves, however, was clearly a first step toward establishing the regulation of employee mobility as a subject of negotiations between management and the union.

The union continued to press for making seniority a deciding factor in decisions to move employees to open jobs. At the end of 1945, after the war had ended, negotiations over the relationship between transfer and seniority broke down, and strikes continued until March 1946, when negotiations were finally concluded.[23]

Phase 4: The March 19, 1946, revision of the agreement

As a result of the strike, the new contract contained the following language concerning employee promotion:

The transferring of employees is solely the responsibility of Management.

(a) In the advancement of employees to higher paid jobs when ability, merit and capacity are equal, employees with the longest seniority will be given preference.

(b) It is the policy of Management to cooperate in every practical way with employees who desire transfers to new positions or vacancies in their department. Accordingly, such employees who make application to their foreman or the Personnel Department stating their desires, qualifications and experiences, will be given preference for openings in their department provided they are capable of doing the jobs. However, employees who have made application as provided for above and who are capable of doing the job available shall be given preference for openings in their department over new hires. Any secondary job openings resulting from filling jobs pursuant to this provision may be filled through promotion; or through transfer without regard to seniority standing; or by new hire.

In plants where departments are too small or in other cases where the number of job classifications within a department is insufficient to permit the practical application of the above paragraph, arrangements whereby employees may make such application for transfer out of their department may be negotiated locally, subject to approval by the Corporation and the International Union.[24]

As seen above, the National Agreement of March 1946 distinguished between promotion, in Sub-Paragraph (a), and transfer, in Sub-Paragraph (b). For non-promotion transfers to new positions and vacancies, management agreed to respect employee preferences as long as the employee was capable of performing the available job. Until this time, the UAW had had no say in employee transfers, so this was a step forward for the union—the first time it was able to influence the transfer of employees.

Furthermore, "in plants where departments are too small," the rules for transfer were to be decided by each factory. This opened up the possibility of transfer between departments. Although transfers to another department based on this provision were infrequent, the option for an employee to request one represented an expansion of employee rights.

From the UAW's viewpoint, two problems remained. First, seniority rights were still not taken into consideration in job transfer decisions. Second, the definition of "transfer" itself was not always clear. For example, when there was a temporary opening, did it fall within the category of transfers?

With room remaining for differing interpretations on these two issues, the union desired to further and more clearly establish seniority as a basis for job transfer decisions. The interpretation of the language of Sub-Paragraph 63 (b) in arbitration decisions made in 1947 exerted a powerful influence on the future direction of transfer rules.

Phase 5: Following the arbitration award of January 13, 1947

The arbitration award of January 13, 1947, covered six similar cases that were settled at the same time.[25] In these rulings, the arbitrator made clear the general interpretation of Sub-Paragraphs 63 (a) and (b). Among these six cases, the most typical was that from the GM's Guide Lamp Division, concerning a grievance filed on May 7, 1946. The complainant was a male employee in the headlamp division, an "Assembler on Head Lamps, Small and Service Parts–Male," who was paid an hourly wage of $1.245. All workers in the headlamp division were paid the same hourly rate, even if there were differences in the content of their work. The complainant informed the foreman of the headlamp door section that when additional soldering work on headlamp doors became available, he would like to be assigned to it. With the installation of two new dial soldering tables, additional soldering work did become available. The grievance alleged, however, that instead of assigning the complainant to this new work, the foreman gave it to other employees with less seniority.

The union appealed, arguing that this violated Sub-Paragraph 63 (b), which governed the transfer of employees. However, in the arbitration decision, it was ruled that this was a change in job assignment, not a transfer, because even though the work content changed, the job classification had not changed. In other words, it was judged that the change of the employee's position was within the same job category and that it was therefore a matter over which management held exclusive authority, not contrary to Paragraph 63. On the basis of this interpretation, the grievance of the employee and the union was dismissed.

To counter the ruling that a transfer within one department and within the same job classification was regarded as a "change of job assignment" and under the exclusive authority of management, the union adopted a strategy of increasing the number of job classifications in order to narrow the scope of management discretion. This countermeasure resulted in the number of job categories increasing to nearly 200 in some plants.

In addition to the above, two additional interpretations were made regarding ambiguous wording in Sub-Paragraph (b). One was that when a transfer order came from a foreman, the employee could not refuse it. The other was that priority is given to promoting an existing employee rather than hiring a new employee for an open job. While these clarifications could not be immediately added to the provisions of the agreement, they were cited and made use of in all future cases of conflict between labor and management concerning these matters. Thus, while this arbitration ruling did not address the role of seniority in non-promotion transfers, it gave rise to several new views regarding the scope and definition of transfer.

Phase 6: The June 12, 1955, revision of the agreement

With the division of Paragraph 63 into Sub-Paragraphs (a) and (b) in the 1946 agreement, the prototype was created that led to today's contract language. Based on the 1946 agreement, the contract language was revised during the negotiations for the 1950 agreement, and important changes were again made in 1955 and 1976.

In the revised agreement of June 12, 1955, the following sentence was added to Sub-Paragraph (b): "In the case the opening is in an equal or lower rated classification and there is more than one applicant capable of doing the job, the applicant with the longest seniority will be given preference."[26] This meant that not only promotion but also employee transfer was now governed by seniority rights, and it gave employees more opportunities to transfer from their current job to a different one.

Phase 7: The November 22, 1976, revision of the agreement until today

In the revised agreement of November 22, 1976, Sub-Paragraph 63 (a) was newly divided into parts (1) and (2).[27] Part (1) contained the conventional rule for promotion within a department, while part (2) was new and covered promotion to other departments. Until this time, promotion to a position outside an employee's original department had been impossible, but this now changed, further expanding opportunities for promotion. For promotions within a department, priority was given to those with the longest seniority if the skills and capabilities of candidates were the same. For promotions to positions outside the employee's department, a new transfer application form was used. In this form applicants wrote their desires, qualifications, and experience when applying for an open position, but the date they started working for the company (which would show their seniority) did not appear in the form. In addition, it was also stipulated that it was possible to apply for up to two job openings outside one's department, using predetermined procedures.

In the subsequent 1979 contract negotiations, modifications were made to the newly prescribed provision, but there was no fundamental change. In negotiations since then, few changes have been made to the language regarding transfers. Thus, the 1976 agreement marks the final phase 7; little change is seen between then and today.

As described above, the area covered by the seniority rights gradually increased as a result of arbitration awards and agreement revision negotiations regarding employee transfer and promotion. There was also an increase in the number of job classifications. It is important to note that further work organization reform represented by the team concept of the 1980s did not affect the provisions of the National Agreement; such more recent reform of work organization mainly affected local agreements. Depending on the progress of work organization reform in the future, it is fully conceivable that the National Agreement will be affected in some way, but this will be a major task imposed on both labor and management.

Conclusion

This chapter has described the development of employee transfer and promotion rules and the expansion of related seniority rights related to these rules up to the present national agreements. During the development process, many labor–management conflicts occurred during contract negotiations and some problems were resolved through arbitration. However, as the years passed, the scope of transfer and promotion was expanded and the use of seniority rights was strengthened, leading to a decrease in the number of arbitration cases. More recent work organization reform issues concerning the transfer and promotion system will be discussed in Chapter 3.

Notes

1 Koike (1976).
2 Shinohara (2003), Chap.5..
3 Gersuny (1982), pp. 521–524.
4 *Ibid.*
5 *Ibid.*
6 Jacoby (1985), pp. 243–246.
7 *Ibid.*
8 *Ibid.*
9 UAW General Motors Department (1950).
10 Gersuny and Kaufman (1985), p. 467.
11 General Motors and the International Union United Automobile Workers of America-C. I. O. (1940), pp. 21-22.
12 Taylor (1941a).
13 Source: past arbitration records collected by the author.
14 On a side note, the following is an example of how many filed grievances progressed to actual arbitration awards. From January 24, 1940 to January 11, 1941, at GM's Chevrolet Division plant in Flint, Michigan, a total of 1,986 grievances were filed by employees in all areas. Of these, 1,374 were settled at the shop floor level through shop committees and negotiations with foremen. Of the rest, 246 were resolved by higher-level sub-committees, 295 by higher-level shop committees, and 69 at the GM company level. This left only two unresolved cases, which were submitted for arbitration. In other words, only about one out of 1,000 filed grievances reached arbitration. These numbers suggest that the 12 job transfer and seniority cases around the 1940 National Agreement that reached arbitration represent a far greater number of filed and processed grievances (WPR Collection, Box 23, File 9, Walter Reuther Library, Wayne State University).
15 General Motors and the International Union United Automobile Workers of America–C.I.O. (1941), p. 66.
16 Taylor (1941b).
17 A reliefman is a person who substitutes for a production worker who takes a leave of absence, or works temporarily in place of a worker who goes to the bathroom. Reliefman was an easy and popular position because they were paid even when they didn't work because no one was on leave.
18 Taylor (1941b).
19 *Ibid.*
20 Taylor (1942); Dash (1942).
21 Kawamura (1995), pp. 180–182.
22 General Motors and the International Union United AutomobileWorkers of America-C. I. O. (1945), p. 63.
23 Lichtenstein (1995), pp. 244-246.
24 General Motors and the International Union United Automobile Workers of America–C.I.O. (1946), pp. 38–39.
25 Seward (1947).
26 General Motors and the International Union United Automobile Workers of America–C.I.O. (1955), pp. 46–48.
27 General Motors and the International Union United Automobile Workers of America–C.I.O. (1976), pp. 46–48.

References

Dash, G., Jr. (1942, February 6). *Umpire Decision B-100*. UAW-GM Umpire Decisions, GM Department, UAW.

General Motors and the International Union United Automobile Workers of America-C. I. O. (1940). *Agreement Between General Motors Corporation and the International Union Automobile Workers of America-C. I. O.*

General Motors and the International Union United Automobile Workers of America-C. I. O. (1941). *Agreement Between General Motors Corporation and the International Union Automobile Workers of America-C. I. O.*

General Motors and the International Union United Automobile Workers of America-C. I. O. (1945). *Agreement Between General Motors Corporation and the International Union Automobile Workers of America-C. I. O.*

General Motors and the International Union United Automobile Workers of America-C. I. O. (1946). *Agreement Between General Motors Corporation and the International Union Automobile Workers of America-C. I. O.*

General Motors and the International Union United Automobile Workers of America-C. I. O. (1955). *Agreement Between General Motors Corporation and the International Union Automobile Workers of America-C. I. O.*

General Motors and the International Union United Automobile Workers of America-C. I. O. (1976). *Agreement Between General Motors Corporation and the International Union Automobile Workers of America-C. I. O.*

Gersuny, Curl. (1982, August). "Origins of Seniority Provisions in Collective Bargaining." *Labor Law Journal*, 33(8), 518–524.

Gersuny, Curl, and G. Kaufman. (1985). "Seniority and the Moral Economy of U. S. Automobile Workers, 1934–1946." *Journal of Social History*, 18(3), 463–475.

Jacoby, Sanford M. (1985). *Employing Bureaucracy: Managers, Unions, and the Transformation of Work in American Industry, 1900–1945*. New York: Columbia University Press.

Kawamura, Tetsuji. (1985). *Pax Amerikana no Keisei*. Tokyo: Toyo Keizai Shinposha.

Koike, Kazuo. (1977). *Shokuba No Rodo Kumiai To Sanka*. Tokyo: Toyo Keizai Shinposha.

Lichtenstein, Nelson. (1995), *The Most Dangerous Man in Detroit: Walter Reuther and the fate of American labor*, New York: Basic Books.

Seward, R. (1947, January 13). *Umpire Decision E-44*. UAW-GM Umpire Decisions, GM Department, UAW.

Shinohara, Kenichi. (2003). *Tenkanki no Amerika Roushikankei*. Kyoto: Minerva Shobo

Taylor, G. (1941a, April 11). *Umpire Decision A-48*, UAW-GM Umpire Decisions, GM Department, UAW.

Taylor, G. (1941b, December 30). *Umpire Decision B-52*, UAW-GM Umpire Decisions, GM Department, UAW.

Taylor, G. (1942, January 12). *Umpire Decision B-69*, UAW-GM Umpire Decisions, GM Department, UAW.

UAW General Motors Department. (1950). *Educational Outline UAW/CIO-GM: National Agreement: Paragraph 63a*.

3 Work organization reform (1)

The case of General Motors Plant A

Introduction

This chapter presents a case study of work organization reform at "Plant A" of General Motors. But as a prelude to the case study, it is important to mention two points. First, it is widely known that work organization in the American automotive industry is built around what Kazuo Koike has termed "obvious rules," that is, rules that "leave no room for misunderstanding."[1] However, areas that are not covered by "obvious rules" have not yet been fully identified and described. One purpose of this case study is to clarify issues in the domain of "non-obvious" work rules.

Second, although work organization reform has been pursued in the US auto industry since the 1980s, the actual situation in unionized plants up until 2009 has not been fully understood, as we have described in Chapter 1. It is important to understand how reforms represented by terms like the "team concept" and "flexibility" are negotiated and agreed on with the union and what specific mechanisms have been adopted to improve productivity. Previous studies have not fully explored Local Agreements (collective bargaining agreements between individual plants and local unions) concerning personnel transfers and the seniority rule, which are inevitably affected by work organization reform.

We will address these points by answering three basic questions, based on our study of US auto plants, especially at GM.[2] The first question is: Which areas of work organization do not have "obvious rules," and what are the important issues in those areas? It is critical to understand the situation that existed up until 2009. For example, one of the most contentious issues raised by workers every year in Big Three auto plants concerns decisions around seniority rights. On the surface, seniority rights would seem to be covered by "obvious rules," but this is not always the case: the issue of seniority rights has created much tension between labor and management.

DOI: 10.4324/9781003282426-3

The second question is: In what form has the "team concept" been implemented and how has it been received by workers in the US auto industry? It is also important to understand the goal(s) of using teams and whether they function effectively.

The third question concerns the relationship between the "team concept" and "obvious rules": How does the introduction of the team concept affect "obvious rules" in the areas of seniority rights and the detailed division and assignment of duties? These three questions are the focus of this case study.

The answers to these questions are influenced by an important difference between work organizations in Japanese and US auto plants, which has been described in Chapter 1. At auto plants in Japan, "continuous improvement" activities are supported by a merit system for "non-routine" work by production workers aimed at reducing waste and inefficiency in operations. Those efforts lead to reductions in man-hours, but workers are not laid off. Conversely, in the United States, it is difficult to see a connection between work organization reform and cost reduction, as strong unions resist the introduction of a merit system for production workers. It has also been very difficult to introduce a clear performance management system through cooperation between the union and management in the United States. In such an environment prior to 2009, with no merit pay for production workers and no strong performance management system, how did labor and management view and deal with work organization reform? The following case study, which focuses on the car body assembly department of GM's Plant A, is based on this perspective. (In the following, the term "workers" refers to unskilled workers in the production department unless otherwise noted.)

Case study of General Motors Plant A

Job transfer mechanisms

In the American automotive industry, collective agreements can be broadly divided into two types: the National Agreement, which is an agreement between GM's headquarters and the United Auto Workers (UAW) headquarters, and Local Agreements between individual plants and their local UAW union, which are only valid at specific plants. At GM's Plant A, significant work organization reform was enacted when the Local Agreement was revised in 1993, including the creation of a seniority rights system with clear rules. However, changes in job classification or job assignment within a department are not subject to regulation under these rules. Few studies have discussed this issue despite the fact that, to this day, the union has no say in changes of job assignment. The reason for this is that most research focuses on the National Agreement, not Local Agreements. As this situation makes clear, it is important to understand the extent to which union regulations are enforced and which areas are not being regulated. Therefore, we have investigated the collective agreements that govern job transfer rules. First, we discuss the National Agreement.

The National Agreement

In the National Agreement, the main provisions regarding transfers are set out in Paragraph (63). Paragraph (63) begins by stating that transfers are solely a management prerogative.[3] It then goes on, in two Sub-Paragraphs, to provide a long description of the collateral conditions that govern transfers.

Sub-Paragraph (63)(a)(1) concerns promotion.[4] It stipulates that when there are multiple candidates for a promotion within a department (e.g., the body department or the paint department) and all have the same ability to perform the job, then the candidate with the most seniority is given prefer-ence. In the case of GM's Plant A, the following stipulation in the National Agreement applied:

> In plants where departments are too small or in other cases where the number of job classifications within a department is insufficient to permit the practical application of this paragraph, arrangements whereby employees may make such application for transfer out of their department may be negotiated locally, subject to approval by the Corporation and the International Union.[5]

Therefore, as of 1995 (the time of an interview survey conducted by the author), promotions were essentially determined solely according to seniority.[6]

Sub-Paragraph (63)(a)(2) concerns promotion to other departments (for example, moving from the body department to the transportation department) within a plant.[7] The number of promotions to other departments was said to be decreasing in the mid-1990s. Plant A did not have a specified promotion route; in principle, people could be promoted anywhere inside or outside their department in accordance with seniority rights.

The next Sub-Paragraph (63)(b), concerns transfers within a department that do not involve a wage rate increase (i.e., transfers that are not promo-tions).[8] The distinction between a "transfer" and a "change in job assign-ment" is important; the former involves moving from one job classification to another job classification and is decided according to seniority, while the latter is a change of position within the same job classification and is decided by management (i.e., the foreman). According to Lichtenstein (1988), in

1945, before the current Sub-Paragraph (63)(b) was established, there was a major dispute between labor and management regarding the definition of a "change in job assignment." Management wanted to define it broadly, so that it could move workers as freely and as widely as possible. The UAW, on the other hand, argued that even a very small change in a worker's position was a "transfer" and therefore governed by seniority, not management. Currently, Sub-Paragraph (63)(b) only covers transfers to a different job classification within a department.

For transfers within a department, the National Agreement stipulates that the transferred employee must be able to perform the work of the transfer destination and that workers who can carry out the work at the destination job are given preference over new recruits. In addition, when an opening is in a classification with an equal or lower wage rate, the person with the longest seniority is given preference.

Another important aspect of job transfers in the American automobile industry that is rarely discussed by researchers is "secondary job openings" that are created when a person who has been performing one job is transferred to a different job. These openings are allocated to workers who have been engaged in other duties in the same department[9] or to new hires. The National Agreement states:

Any secondary job openings resulting from filling jobs pursuant to this provision may be filled through promotions; or through transfer without regard to seniority standing, or by new hire.

According to a UAW official, Plant A did not originally rely on promotions to fill secondary job openings. Except in the case of new hires, transfers were determined solely by management. That is, transfers to primary job openings were effectively determined by seniority rights, but transfers to secondary job openings were made at the discretion of the on-site foreman.[10] However, as of 2009, disagreement between labor and management on this point was said to remain at Plant A because, according to the union, foremen often base promotion decisions on who they like rather than on more objective criteria.

The Local Agreement

At GM Plant A, a new regulation on changes of job assignment was added to the Local Agreement in 1993. Before this, the foreman had total authority over changes in job assignments. But in the 1993 agreement the union succeeded in gaining a say in job transfers for the first time at this plant. The relevant article is Paragraph (304) of the Local Agreement, which covers "Intra-department job selection transfers."[11] We investigated several other Local Agreements and

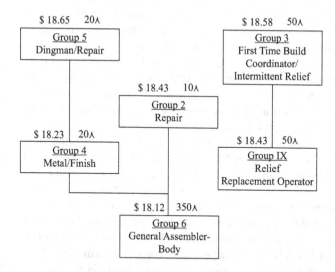

Figure 3.1 Relationship among occupation groups in body department and representative hourly wage rate and worker numbers for each (1993) (Source: Lansing Car Assembly, Body and Local 602, U.A.W., *Local Agreement between Lansing Car Assembly, Body Plant and Local 602, U.A.W. (October 1993)*).

could not find any with clear stipulations regarding changes of job assignment.[12] This shows that the union has greater control over the workplace in Plant A than in other plants. In most plants, as of 2009, it seems that position changes were essentially at the foreman's discretion.

Figure 3.1 illustrates the transfer procedure described in Paragraph (304), taking general assembly workers (Group 6) as an example. When there is a job opening, the worker who has the most seniority within the same classification, occupational group, department, and shift, and who is capable of performing the duties associated with the open job, has the right to apply for that opening preferentially. In other words, if the worker with the most seniority desires to move, he is automatically chosen under these conditions. However, if he does not desire to move, the right to apply for the open job goes to the worker with the second-most seniority. If this worker wants to transfer to the open job, then he or she can. Similarly, if this worker does not want to transfer, the right to apply for the job opening is transferred to the worker with the third-highest seniority, and so on. In this way, the right to apply for a job opening descends on order of seniority. If no qualified person is available, then, according to Paragraph (63)(a)(b) of the National Agreement and

Paragraph (306) (provisions for "Intra-departmental transfers") of the Local Agreement (described below), the foreman can decide who fills the position. As position changes were previously determined unilaterally by the foreman, this example provides a good illustration of the union's success in restricting the absolute authority of management in the workplace.

In exchange for allowing job transfers to be determined by seniority rather than the decision of the foreman, GM management sought, in the 1993 Local Agreement negotiations, to significantly reduce the number of job classifications.[13] Such a reduction progressed simultaneously with the implementation of the team concept, as described below.

After the 1993 Local Agreement, with the introduction of teamwork at Plant A, the number of job classifications decreased, and seniority-based promotions to higher-paying job classifications became more difficult. The purpose of reducing the number of job classifications and introducing team-work was to broaden workers' skills and knowledge by having them flexibly engage in a wider range of tasks instead of being confined to a limited set of duties. As is discussed further in this book, this effort is still ongoing under GMS (GM's Global Manufacturing System). A critical obstacle to achieving this, and to gaining contributions from workers in the form of suggestions for continuous improvement, has been the inability to introduce elements of meritocracy into the worker evaluation system.

The inter-department transfer procedure (for example, moving from the body department to the trim department) has been part of the Local Agreement for some time. This procedure is described in Paragraph (306) of the Local Agreement. Transfers to other departments are permitted as long as seniority rights are satisfied, so workers can be transferred within a fairly wide range of jobs of their own volition. But it is not a general practice for workers to be steadily promoted within their department.

The team concept and work organization reform

Simplification of job classifications

(1) BEFORE THE LOCAL AGREEMENT EXPIRED IN 1990

The primary task of the body department is to weld car bodies. Although job classifications within departments were consolidated in the 1993 Local Agreement, no changes were made to the job classifications in previous agreements.[14]

Figure 3.2 shows the relationship among occupational groups in the body department at Plant A, including wage rates for each group. The higher the occupational group, the higher the wage rate. Vertical lines connecting occupational groups represent personnel "bumping" paths during layoffs, not paths of promotion. As mentioned above, promotions do not

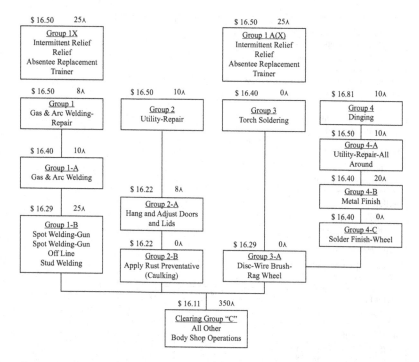

Figure 3.2 Relationship among occupation groups in body department and representative hourly wage rate and worker numbers for each (1990) (Source: Lansing Car Assembly, Body and Local 602, U.A.W., *Local Agreement between Lansing Car Assembly, Body Plant and Local 602, U.A.W. (October 1990)*).

follow a single fixed route but can occur widely within and outside a department through seniority rights. If a layoff is to take place, workers are laid off in the order of least seniority, starting from the lowest level, which is Clearing Group C (all other body shop operations). Employees who belong to Clearing Group C have shorter service lengths than employees in other occupational groups.

Under the job classification system that was in place until the 1990 Local Agreement expired, at Plant A the body department alone had 15 occupational groups (see Figure 3.2). According to the 1990 Local Agreement, the entire plant had 95 occupational groups, including skilled and unskilled occupational groups. Moreover, each occupational group was divided into several job classifications. Figure 3.3 shows the occupational groups in the assembly department and job classifications within each group in 1993, after the reduction in the number of job classifications. At this time, as

	Rate
RateDingman-Repair (Utility Repair All Around-18.43) (Dinging-18.65)	18.65
Repair (Gas & Arc Weld Repair-18.43) (Gas & Arc Weld-18.43) (Utility Repair-18.43)	18.43
Intermittent Relief (Intermittent Relief 1X-18.43) (Intermittent Relief 1AX-18.43)	18.43
Relief (Relief 1AX-18.43) (Relief 1X-18.43)	18.43
Replacement Operator (Absentee Replacement 1AX-18.43) (Absentee Replacement 1X-18.43)	18.43
Metal Finish (Metal Finish-18.43)	18.23
Body Assembler (Spot Weld-Gun-18.12) (Spot Weld-Off Line-18.12) (Stud Weld-18.12) (Hang & Adjust Doors & Lids-18.12) (Disc-Wire Brush-18.12) (Bolt & Drill-17.93) (Apply Sealer-17.93) (Booking Desk-18.12)	18.12

Figure 3.3 Occupational groups in body department (bold type), job classifications within each group (in parentheses), and hourly wage rates (1993) (Source: Lansing Car Assembly, Body and Local 602, U.A.W., *Local Agreement between Lansing Car Assembly, Body Plant and Local 602, U. A. W. (October 1993)*).

explained above, job position changes, which had previously been decided by the foreman, were regulated by seniority rights according to Paragraph 304 of the Local Agreement.

(2) JOB CLASSIFICATION AND WAGE RATES AFTER THE LOCAL AGREEMENT OF 1993

The 15 occupational groups of the body department in the 1990 agreement were reduced to seven in 1993 (see Figure 3.3).[15] With the simplification and integration of occupational groups, management aimed to make it easier to move employees within an occupational group. However, in the local contract negotiations, the union succeeded in adding regulations in Paragraph 304 of the Local Agreement that made changes of job assignment within a job classification, previously a prerogative of management, subject to seniority rights. The union was also interested in exploring the team concept, which was introduced along with the reduction in occupational groups.

In the 1993 Local Agreement, the lowest level of general assembly work, Clearing Group C in 1990 and Group 6 in 1993, experienced no change in terms of the number of workers or positions within the department.[16] The occupational groups that were combined were those at higher positions. As in the 1990 agreement, higher occupational groups have higher wage rates. But the wage gap between higher and lower occupational groups within a department shrank relative to the 1990 agreement, and so relatively older employees with greater seniority became less likely to seek promotions.[17] Rather than seeking promotion for a slight increase in wages, these employees tended to move to simpler jobs off the production line. However, the number of off-line positions was decreasing.

The 1993 agreement simplified the vertical lines connecting different occupational groups, and the bumping (displacement transfer) mechanism for layoffs or employee reductions also became simpler.[18] Employees in Group 3 of Figure 3.1 are the so-called team leaders introduced in the 1993 agreement. (In the plant, the team concept was also called "First Time Build," and leaders were called "coordinators.") Group 1X, located below the team leader, also played a major role in receiving surplus personnel from the greatly reduced environmental services department. The environmental services department was mainly responsible for cleaning the interior of the plant. Many workers thought that these jobs were relatively easy because all the work was performed off the assembly line; therefore, this occupational group was a popular transfer destination. Thus, when employees were moved out of the environmental services department, which had many senior workers, to other departments, they could immediately take team leader or assistant type jobs in the destination department, owing to their higher seniority.[19]

Team concept: "First Time Build"

At GM Plant A, the team concept was introduced in the 1993 Local Agreement and implemented under the name "First Time Build." First Time Build was positioned and pushed forward as a "Quality of Work Life" (QWL) initiative.

A team leader (called a "First Time Build coordinator" in the Local Agreement) was selected, based on ability, whose primary role was to assist team members, promote communication within the team, and drive the team to carry out the continuous improvement. At the time, the team leader's hourly wage was $18.58, which was not so high compared to the other jobs. Team leaders were given the existing job classification of "intermittent relief," and the previous job classification of "utility" was abolished.

The size of a working team was essentially no more than ten people.[20] Team members were expected to perform a wide range of tasks, not just the tasks that were specific to particular job classification. However, an examination of the recommended roles of team members leaves the impression that the team concept ideals are generally accepted ideals in the United States. For example, these ideals include helping other team members, communicating within the team about quality and cost, voluntarily taking responsibility for employee involvement, participating in the suggestion system, and attending problem-solving meetings. The system relied heavily on voluntary participation by workers. It was also expected that workers would demonstrate autonomy through teamwork, leading to cost reductions and quality improvements. In this sense, this team concept was very optimistic.

Moreover, as part of the wide range of jobs within a team, the task of keeping the work area clean was added.[21] Originally, such cleaning work was the exclusive job of the environmental services department, but the size of this department was reduced significantly in the 1993 agreement. This change made it unclear which cleaning tasks were to be performed within the team and which were the responsibility of the environmental services department.[22] In any case, the team concept at this time can be described as immature and unstable.[23] Team members reportedly received only 40 hours of training over a three-year period, which was insufficient.

One important task of a team leader was to fill in when team members were absent.[24] This usually meant doing regular line work. The reason is that this plant was not hiring new workers in those days, and as a result there was a chronic shortage of workers and a high absenteeism rate. During the three years covered by the 1996 Local Agreement (1996–1998), team leaders received 72 hours of training. However, covering the duties of absent workers required substantial training.

When the First Time Build concept was introduced, some team members and team leaders understood it well and accepted it positively, but many employees did not.[25]

Unlike traditional QWL initiatives, the team activities within First Time Build involved greater worker participation in quality and production processes than before, and in that sense more focus on production activities was required.[26] If a formal working team meeting was held after hours, the workers received a salary supplement for participating in it. Attendance at problem-solving meetings was essentially up to each individual team member. As far as circumstances allowed, the holding of and attendance at meetings was at the discretion of each team. Many teams reported had a weekly 20-minute meeting as an easy method of contact, but these meetings included no discussion of problem-solving or issues.[27]

Both labor and management agreed that the training of team members was important for making First Time Build more active.[28] Therefore, employees received technical training, and three stages of wage increases were established depending on the level of skill acquired.[29] These wage stages reflect so-called "pay-for-skill." As already mentioned, the wage rate for general production workers was $18.12 (level 1). However, by acquiring and demonstrating mastery of additional skills, a worker could raise his wage rate to Level 2 (meaning that the worker can perform two job types; $18.23) or Level 3 (meaning that the worker can perform all job types in the team; $18.44). In practice, however, this system did not function as intended: only 1% of employees reached Level 2 and 0% reached Level 3.[30] Even if workers learned additional skills, their wages did not increase significantly, providing little motivation.

Interestingly, in connection with wage increases due to skills acquisition, if one team member did not wish to have his skills evaluated (skill evaluations were carried out by a team of six to eight co-workers), his wish was respected.[31] It is difficult to interpret this finding with certainty, but we can easily imagine that this would not occur in a Japanese workplace. Under First Time Build at Plant A, whether a new improvement activity or a proposal system was pursued, its success depended on the individual contribution of each worker, but most workers did not contribute as hoped. Thus, obstacles that arose in practice prevented the team concept as described in the agreement from functioning effectively.

An additional problem at Plant A was that voluntary job rotation did not occur, with one exception: for ergonomic reasons to reduce the occurrence of injuries. It was said that job rotation blurs the principle of job ownership, which is the underlying principle of the worker wage structure.[32] The fact that job rotation was impossible in principle, along with the fact that pay-for-skill did not function effectively, meant that the role of the team concept was very limited.

The changing role of the foreman

Before the 1993 Local Agreement, the foreman had substantial authority. Reports indicate that each foreman monitored only 20 to 30 employees, and so supervision was close.[33] Also, as previously mentioned, position transfers were determined solely at the foreman's discretion.

With the adoption of Paragraph 304 of the 1993 Local Agreement, the foreman's discretionary power over job assignments became more restricted, and his role in deciding the placement of subordinate workers diminished. With the 1993 Local Agreement, the number of employees monitored by each foreman increased significantly, to between 50 and 80.[34] With this change, the primary role of the foreman also expanded: from employee monitoring to also including coaching and advising. Foremen also received training in problem-solving in the production process, and in the future they were expected to assist their teams in solving problems. Foremen also had to negotiate with the team leaders, which was another new aspect of their job.

Summary

We summarize and conclude this chapter with the following three points.

First, we have clarified which areas are and are not governed by regulations in the work organization of Plant A. Changes in job assignment, which were traditionally determined at the foreman's discretion, came to be determined by seniority rights; this was something the local union had been demanding for many years. However, no regulations were in place regarding the filling of secondary job openings; this issue remains a point of discussion between labor and management.

Second, in exchange for the new regulations on job assignment changes, the plant management won the introduction of the team concept. At first, the union cooperated with the introduction of the team concept, which had been a major topic since the 1980s, with the hope that it would make the workplace more "democratic."

Third, although the team concept was introduced, there were a number of challenges, including (1) the inability to motivate individual workers, (2) the inability to transfer or relocate workers freely, and (3) a lack of clear awareness of how the team concept can lead to increased productivity.

Due to these three factors, we conclude that the team concept had a little visible positive effect in the years following its introduction. However, efforts to make it more effective continued until 2009, when GM experienced bankruptcy. In the next chapter, we examine the next stage in the struggle for work organization reform at GM.

Notes

1 Koike (1977), p. 60.
2 Shinohara (2003), Chap. 1.

3 UAW and General Motors Corporation (1993), pp. 46–48.
4 *Ibid.*, p. 46.
5 *Ibid.*, p. 49.
6 Author's interview with officer at local A of UAW (November 19, 1995).
7 UAW and General Motors Corporation, *op. cit.*, pp. 46–47.
8 *Ibid.*, pp. 47–48.
9 UAW and General Motors Corporation, *op. cit.*, p. 48.
10 Author's email exchange with officer at local A of UAW (September 18, 1998).
11 Lansing Car Assembly, Body Plant and Local 602, U.A.W. (1993), pp. 175–178.
12 Other Local Agreements investigated: Local 594, U.A.W. and North American Truck Platform-Pontiac, General Motors Corporation (1993), Local 599, U.A.W. and Nao-Flint Complex (Buick City), General Motors Corporation (1993), Local 900, U.A.W. and Wayne Body & Stamping, Ford Motor Company (1990).
13 Author's email exchange with officer at local A of UAW (September 18, 1996).
14 Lansing Car Assembly, Body Plant and Local 602, U.A.W. (1990), p. 12.
15 Lansing Car Assembly, Body Plant and Local 602, U.A.W., *op. cit.*, November 1993, p. 12.
16 Author's interview with officer at local A of UAW (December 19, 1995).
17 Author's email exchange with officer at local A of UAW (October 16, 1996).
18 Author's interview with officer at local A of UAW (December 19, 1995).
19 *Ibid.*
20 Lansing Car Assembly, Body Plant and Local 602, U.A.W., *op. cit.*, November 1993, p. 79.
21 *Ibid.*, pp. 83–84.
22 Author's interview with officer at local A of UAW (November 19, 1995).
23 Author's email exchange with officer at local A of UAW (October 16, 1996).
24 Lansing Car Assembly, Body Plant and Local 602, U.A.W., *op. cit.*, November 1993, pp. 80–81.
25 Author's email exchange with officer at local A of UAW (October 16, 1996).
26 Lansing Car Assembly, Body Plant and Local 602, U.A.W., *op. cit.*, November 1993, p. 80.
27 Author's email exchange with officer at local A of UAW (October 16, 1996).
28 Lansing Car Assembly, Body Plant and Local 602, U.A.W., *op. cit.*, November 1993, p. 80.
29 *Ibid.*, November, 51993, p. 87.
30 Author's interview with officer at local A of UAW (November 19, 1995).
31 Author's email exchange with officer at local A of UAW (October 16, 1996).
32 *Ibid.*
33 *Ibid.*
34 *Ibid.*

References

General Motors and the International Union United Automobile Workers of America-C. I. O. (1990). *Agreement Between General Motors Corporation and the International Union Automobile Workers of* America-C. I. O.
General Motors and the International Union United Automobile Workers of America-C. I. O. (1993). *Agreement Between General Motors Corporation and the International Union Automobile Workers of* America-C. I. O.

50 *Work organization reform (1)*

Koike, Kazuo. (1977). *Shokuba No Rodo Kumiai To Sanka.* Tokyo: Toyo Keizai Shinposha.

Lansing Car Assembly, Body Plant and Local 602, U. A. W. (1990). *Local Agreement Between Lansing Car Assembly, Body Plant and Local 602, U. A. W.*

Lansing Car Assembly, Body Plant and Local 602, U. A. W. (1993). *Local Agreement Between Lansing Car Assembly, Body Plant and Local 602, U. A. W.*

Lichtenstein, Nelson. (1988). "The Union's Early Days: Shop Steward and Seniority." Mike Paker and Jane Slautghter (eds.), *Choosing Sides: Union and the Team Concept.* Boston: South End Press.

Shinohara, Kenichi. (2003). *Tenkanki no Amerika Roushikankei,* Kyoto: Minerva Shobo.

4 Work organization reform at General Motors (2)

Introduction

The purpose of this chapter is to describe GM's efforts to introduce work organization reform during the years leading up to and following the automaker's bankruptcy in 2009. Obliged by the terms of the bankruptcy agreement to restructure its plant management, organizational reform efforts evolved from the simple "team concept" to more specific actions aimed at improving productivity and quality. Some of GM's plant management initiatives were successful, but others failed to work well for a variety of reasons.

There is an often-told anecdote about inefficiencies in American automobile plants. A light bulb goes out in a particular workshop, and a worker there calls the electrician. The electrician confirms that the light bulb has burned out, but before he can replace it, he needs to call a mechanic to remove the lampshade. The mechanic is called, but he is on a coffee break. When he returns and checks the light, he discovers a broken wiring pipe, so he has to call a plumber before removing the lampshade. In this way, time continues to pass. This story is meant as a humorous illustration of wastefulness at an auto plant, but such situations are actually all too common.

The continuous improvement activities that are often carried out in production plants in Japan are a mechanism for workers to permanently solve problems of "wastefulness," or *muda* in Japanese. *Muda* includes unnecessary transportation, inventory, motion, and waiting; overproduction and over processing; and defects. It is natural that management at Detroit's Big Three automakers also wanted to reduce wastefulness.[1]

Misunderstanding of "team," overlooking of merit

The management method used in the Japanese automobile industry is known as lean production, or just-in-time (JIT) production, and in the 1980s the idea that labor in Japan's auto industry was based on teams (small groups)

DOI: 10.4324/9781003282426-4

became widely established. Because of the international success of Japanese manufacturers in the 1970s and 1980s, particularly in the automobile and electronics industries, numerous social science researchers studied the Japanese corporate environment and Japanese management methods attracted much attention among consultants and business practitioners. But when American companies tried to adopt Japanese manufacturing methods, the results were often unsatisfactory. A large part of the reason for this was a misunderstanding of the team concept and a failure to appreciate the role of meritocracy in Japanese firms.

In the 1980s, there was much discussion among researchers in the United States regarding the team concept.[2] Japanese teamwork was often seen to be a manifestation of "collectivism," a Japanese cultural value that prioritizes the group over the self. As applied to the workplace, the team concept was understood to mean that when employees work together in teams, it increases satisfaction and communication in the workplace and thereby increases productivity (efficiency) and quality. This understanding was influenced by 1970s research on teamwork at the Kalmar and Uddevalla plants of Swedish automaker Volvo, where the aim was "the humanization of work," in contrast to automobile production based on flow operations connected by an assembly line.[3] Similarly, in the United States many people argued that working together in a group, as opposed to individuals working alone performing a single task, makes work more interesting and satisfying, activates the workplace, and improves efficiency. However, the notion that the Japanese team concept is synonymous with collectivism or "humanizing" the workplace by getting away from the traditional production line is a misunderstanding.

In Japanese auto plants, the team concept is closely connected to the relatively ambiguous boundaries, or overlap, between jobs. Under such a system, even ordinary employees have a relatively large amount of room for creativity and innovation through continuous improvement and quality circle activities. This kind of workplace is difficult to replicate in American auto plants because job descriptions are very specific and pay rates are tied to the particular job an employee performs. In an American auto plant, the tasks to be performed are very clearly defined, and if an employee fails to perform them, he or she is subject to disciplinary action. Perversely, not only is it unnecessary for a worker to perform additional tasks beyond those in his/her job description, but doing more tasks than prescribed is considered an infringement on the work of others. Under such a system, there is little room for creativity and ingenuity on the part of an ordinary worker.

Many American researchers in the 1980s observed Japanese workplaces, but because many of their observations were superficial, and due to their focus on teams, they failed to notice and appreciate the "meritocracy" principle, which is fundamental to Japanese manufacturing. In Japan, production workers who are evaluated as "excellent" can be internally promoted to higher positions and different types of jobs. In contrast, internal promotions for production workers beyond the factory floor are rare in the US auto industry.

Meritocratic treatment is indispensable for motivating individuals to be creative and enhancing their skills and productivity. Overlooking the role that meritocracy plays in Japanese auto plants meant that attempts by US automakers to adopt Japanese-style manufacturing methods were missing a critical element of success.

Production efficiency

In Japanese auto plants, the merit principle is most strongly seen in non-routine (irregular) work. In "routine" work, such as repetitive line work where tasks are highly specified, there is little difference in performance among individual workers. But in "non-routine" work, such as continuous improvement activities, the ideas, innovativeness, and results differ from one employee to another. These differences are reflected in promotions, with high-performing workers being promoted to higher positions. Such merit-based promotions are a critical element of the continuous improvement process for two reasons. First, the merit system (with the potential reward of promotion) encourages production workers to innovate and to make continuous improvements which reduce the number of man-hours needed for production. Second, because high-performing (innovative) production workers are promoted to higher positions, the number of production workers can be reduced without the occurrence of layoffs. Thus, As seen in Figure 4.1, the continuous improvement mechanism is "meritocracy → continuous improvement → reduction of man-hours → reduction of production personnel," and this mechanism does not require laying off production workers.

In US auto plants, it is far more difficult to introduce such a continuous improvement system. First, in the US system, there is no place for "non-routine" work; wages are tied to performing clearly defined, assigned routine jobs, so there is no motivation for workers to do any additional non-routine work. In fact, union rules do not allow a worker to perform work outside his or her narrowly defined job description. Second, because there is no system of internal promotion of production workers in US auto plants, continuous improvement that reduces the number of needed man-hours would lead to layoffs, which workers and the union strongly resist.

Because of these difficulties, the "meritocracy → continuous improvement → reduction of man-hours → reduction of production personnel" system does not work easily at US plants. Instead, a top-down

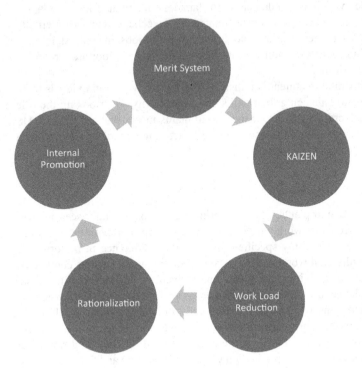

Figure 4.1 The continuous improvement cycle in Japanese automakers. 1. Merit
system in the workplace makes it possible to conduct kaizen activities.
2. Kaizen activities led to a reduction in man-hours. 3. Reduced man-
hours leads to a reduction in necessary personnel. 4. Reduced personnel
does not mean layoffs, as excellent operators can now get promoted. 5.
Promotion reinforces the merit system.

mechanism of "reduction of man-hours → reduction of personnel" has traditionally been used. This mechanism is known as "job combination."

Job combination

In the 1970s, pressures on US automakers to raise productivity were not
strong, and the auto companies had surplus personnel. This changed in
the 1980s, however, with the intensification of international competition,
particularly from Japanese automakers. As US automakers benchmarked
Japanese auto companies in the United States, they became more aggressive
in pursuing "job combination." Job combination refers to combining multiple production line processes into a smaller number of processes which
require less time, and fewer workers, to perform.

In 1990, Detroit's Big Three—GM, Ford, and Chrysler—began to adopt lean production. To do this they created a new position of "team leader"; the job of a team leader was to bring together several production workers to find ways to improve efficiency. Team leader was not a management position, however, because team leaders were union members. Top management wanted to position the team leader as a key player in workplace reform, but foremen and superintendents, who were higher in rank than team leaders, resisted this because it meant that their own work would be taken away. This resistance from middle management made it difficult to achieve efficiency improvements and implement job combinations involving general production workers.

Industrial engineers (IEs) were in charge of planning job combinations. They began by measuring the time it took for workers to perform different production tasks or processes. They sometimes tried to do this inconspicuously, hiding behind pillars with their stopwatches, but when workers realized what they were doing, they responded by intentionally working more slowly, to prevent their workload from being increased later. At such times, this led labor and management to become suspicious of each other and did not foster an atmosphere of cooperation to improve the workplace.

Another problem was that American IEs—unlike Japanese engineers, who frequently visited the shop floor and talked with production workers—worked exclusively in their offices at computers, devising job combinations that would reduce the number of man-days needed to produce an automobile. (One man-day is a unit reflecting the work performed by one person in one day.) Engineers sometimes called foremen to their office to advise them about how they could make changes in the process list, the so-called ALBS (Assembly Line Balance Sheet), to reduce man-days of work. Because the engineers' instructions were based on armchair theories, not hands-on experience at the production line, they were often impractical. Some foremen expressed disapproval when they received such job combination proposals from engineers, but because they were subordinate to the engineers, they had little choice but to try to implement the engineer's instructions on the shop floor. In many cases the foremen received complaints from production workers or found that the suggested job combinations simply failed. This contributed to distrust between management and labor.

This atmosphere of mutual distrust began to gradually change starting in the 1990s. This change was triggered by the introduction of "product development teams" (PDTs), cross-functional teams created for new vehicle launches involving the production and technical departments. With the PDT, new vehicle launches, which had previously been the responsibility of engineers, now involved collaboration with production workers. During new vehicle launches, workers came to personally know the IEs, with whom they had previously had little contact. In this way, the PDTs increased communication between production workers and engineering departments, and trust between the two groups improved as a result. PDTs are discussed in greater detail below.

Continuous improvement to make work easier

The purpose of continuous improvement, as traditionally practiced by Detroit's Big Three, and supported by the UAW, was to make work easier for the existing workforce, not to reduce the number of needed workers. For example, if ten workers were performing various processes, and the production layout was changed to simplify the processes, that meant that the ten workers could work with greater ease because the processes had become simpler. But it did not necessarily mean that the workforce would be reduced to nine people because ten were no longer necessary. Thus, in the United States, "continuous improvement" was separate from "job combination." The former allowed the ten workers to continue working with a lighter workload, while the latter reduced the workforce from ten people to nine.

In general, methods for reducing the number of production line processes in Japan are classified into the following three groups: (1) pure job combinations; (2) reductions in man-hours through continuous improvements, such as creating auxiliary devices; and (3) automation. It is important to understand how conventional wisdom regarding this classification differs between Japan and the Big Three.

According to interviews, in the United States, job combinations and continuous improvements are considered two separate categories. Job combinations are the purview of engineers, whereas continuous improvements entail offering rewards to workers so that they generate ideas. From the union's point of view, there are two problems with job combinations: first, they reduce the number of workers needed, and second, combining two processes into one is seen as creating unfamiliar tasks and making jobs "tighter" and more difficult to perform. Conversely, continuous improvements are clearly different because they make work easier. For this reason, it is easy to implement continuous improvements at the Detroit automakers but difficult to reach agreements with the union regarding job combinations.

In Japan, on the other hand, continuous improvements and job combinations can be grouped together, because when they lead to a reduction in the number of needed workers, excess workers can be promoted to other positions or relocated instead of being dismissed.

Continuous improvement initiatives and the kaizen shop

The Japanese word for continuous improvement, "kaizen," has become so popular in the United States that it is commonly used at factories. Kaizen refers to continuous improvement activities centered on production workers taking the initiative to improve efficiency, health, safety, and quality. The practice of kaizen was developed in the Japanese manufacturing industry and then spread to the United States and other countries.

In the United States, kaizen was first adopted at New United Motor Manufacturing, Inc. (NUMMI), a joint venture between Toyota and GM launched in the early 1980s. NUMMI was located in GM's Fremont, California plant, which had closed in the late 1970s. At NUMMI, Toyota was in charge of plant management and GM was in charge of sales. Eighty percent of the workers who had been laid off when the former GM Fremont plant closed were rehired at the start of operations. The Toyota production system employed at NUMMI has had a large impact on auto plants in the United States and around the world.

Automobile production at NUMMI reached very high quality and productivity levels compared to the former GM Fremont plant, a fact that was reported by John Krafcik, an MIT graduate student who actually worked at NUMMI and conducted a study based on his experience.[4] Krafcik's report received much attention in the United States. (Krafcik joined Korea's Hyundai Motor America in 2009 where he held the positions of President and CEO until 2013.)

In addition to kaizen, the Toyota production system, including *andon* and just-in-time manufacturing, was implemented at NUMMI for the first time in the United States. (*Andon* is a Japanese term meaning "light" or "lamp." In lean production, an andon cord is a tool that is used to alert workers of problems within their production process.) When NUMMI opened in 1984, GM managers and labor representatives went to inspect the NUMMI site, but it took some time for them to grasp the subtle differences in this new production system.

For example, when GM executives asked where the parking lot was for vehicles that needed repair, the NUMMI side answered that there were no parking spaces for repairs. GM executives could not believe this, so they searched Fremont in the middle of the night, thinking that the parking spaces had to be somewhere.

In the Toyota production system, wastefulness, including inventory, is kept to a minimum. A car consists of about 30,000 parts. At US automakers, several months' supply of each part is stocked at a plant, requiring a very large stockyard to store the parts. With just-in-time manufacturing, however, parts and units are sent from suppliers and arrive at the assembly line as needed. The GM executives were similarly surprised when they could find no large inventory stockyard at NUMMI.

Based on what executives saw at NUMMI, in the late 1980s GM established a special task force called the "synchronous workshop" at "Plant A" in Michigan, for the purpose of making production more efficient by reducing the number of processes. The attitude of the union toward the synchronous workshop was ambivalent, however, as workers were not yet accustomed to carrying out reforms through collaboration with management. Given the opposition from workers, union officials feared that if they collaborated with management they would lose their positions in the next union election. It took a long time for production and skilled trades workers to gradually accept the idea of activities that involved cooperation with management. Management also struggled to adjust to the new direction that aimed to involve union members in making changes to improve the assembly process.

More successful in terms of labor–management cooperation was the establishment of another task force, the "kaizen shop," in the late 1990s. The kaizen shop is a specialized team of "improvement professionals" that focuses on improvement activities, in contrast to the synchronous workshop, which tried to involve general production workers in improvement activities. NUMMI was the first GM plant to establish a kaizen shop; they were later set up at other GM plants, but the operational results varied from plant to plant.

In Japan, plants have "continuous improvement teams" of improvement specialists that play a major role in significant improvements, but general production workers are also urged to participate in improvement activities. Production workers are encouraged to participate in improvement activities in the United States as well, but their involvement is lower than it is in Japan. The reason for this difference is that US production workers receive predetermined job-based wages, and non-routine work, such as improvements, is not reflected in their wages. In this way, the non-meritocratic wage system for production workers in the US auto industry works against worker-centered process improvement.

According to interviews, GM's kaizen shops work as follows. There are two teams, one for the day shift and one for the night shift. A team consists of ten workers: two skilled trades workers (i.e., indirect production workers with special skills) from each of four job types—electrician, plumber, mill-wright, and toolmaker—plus two production workers. Each team is divided into two sub-teams, one in charge of the assembly workshop and one in charge of the body and painting workshops. General production workers who want to join the kaizen shop must submit an application, and the Department Quality Council selects the workers in a joint labor–management effort.

In sum, GM wanted to pursue continuous improvements, but because of the difficulty of involving general production workers in improvement activities, a dedicated improvement activity unit called the kaizen shop was developed and put into practice.

Product development teams (PDT)

Figure 4.2 shows the GM organization chart for Plant A. At first glance, the organization charts of GM plants are not much different from those of Toyota. However, the top-down style of GM and the bottom-up style of Toyota mean that employees have different roles at the field level.

Originally, the management style of GM was top-down and engineer-oriented. But influenced by NUMMI, some GM managers made efforts to adopt parts of the Japanese style of labor–management relations, which is more bottom-up and production worker-oriented. The Product Development

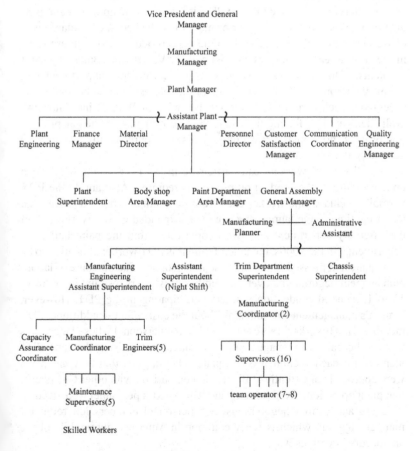

Figure 4.2 Simplified organizational chart of GM.

Team (PDT) from the 1990s was one of these efforts. The PDT was an attempt to use the spirit of labor–management cooperation to improve production line efficiency, which previously had been under the unilateral control of IEs.

Production efficiency is especially important when organizing the processes for launching a new vehicle or after a model change. Once a new model enters mass production, it is difficult to make major changes to the production process. This is especially true because, as described above, the union essentially opposes the introduction of job combinations and new automation that would reduce the number of union members.[5] Thus, because the production processes for a new vehicle or a new model are reorganized from scratch, significant change is possible only before launch. Traditionally, IEs unilaterally determined the organization of production, but production workers have been involved in this process since the 1990s, through PDTs.

Our interviews indicate that the PDT is a team made up of IEs and production workers. When a new car or model is launched, the standard tasks of workers that must be entered into the mass production system are summarized in an easy-to-understand list called "Visual Line Balancing Wall Elements." This list is hung on the wall in the workers' support center in the plant. Before the PDT, workers had little interest in tasks beyond those specified in their own job descriptions. But with the Visual Line Balancing Wall Elements list, for the first time, the entire picture of the car production process (previously known only to IEs) was purposefully disclosed to general production workers.

Not all general workers can participate in the PDT. Naturally, a deep understanding of the production process is required. At Plant A, the PDT normally included one worker each from the paint and body departments, but at the time of the launch, the team was expanded to four workers from the assembly department and two people each from the paint and body departments. In the 2000s, the union found this PDT worker allocation to be inadequate and pressed for an increase in personnel. The outcome of labor–management negotiations over the number of workers resulted in, at most, 10 to 15 general production workers participating in the PDT. However, Plant A's management was unhappy about the costs of these additional PDT members; PDT workers represented additional personnel whose labor costs were to be paid by management, so management insisted that one PDT member for each section was adequate. They argued that new car plans were approved consistently at Plant A in comparison with other GM plants, that plant operations were smooth, and that no extra personnel were needed.

These and similar negotiations over personnel numbers left room for number juggling, which is fairly common in American automobile plants and occurs in various ways.

Unclear plant performance indicators and number juggling

According to interviews, in the negotiations between labor and management over the number of general workers included in the PDT, number juggling was practiced. For example, additional general workers would be added to the PDT in June and then, on paper only, be returned to their original workshops in December and then returned to the PDT in January. This manipulation benefited both sides: it satisfied the union's demand for more general workers on the PDT, while at the same time it allowed management to meet workforce management goals (and impress headquarters with their ability to keep costs down) because the end-of-the-year number of PDT members was (artificially) low. This practice occurred frequently.

Number juggling was related to another issue: plant executives often did not accurately know the numbers of workers in their plants. Personnel management was somewhat complicated owing to the existence of various job types. There were workers from the Jobs Bank,[6] workers who were temporarily assigned to other plants, and workers on sick leave (who were removed from the list of active workers). In short, the situation was that a manager might not know exactly how many people were working at his own plant. As an extension of this unclear personnel management, plants had substantial room for "numerical adjustments" regarding the number of workers. This made it possible for managers to come up with employee numbers that achieve personnel planning targets but did not match actual employee numbers. Such tricks could also be used to create artificial (on paper only) cost reductions. Stakeholders called these "magic numbers" or, when the tricks were performed at the end of the year, "Christmas miracles." The union side often had numbers that differ from those of management.

In particular, at the end of the year, the management side tried to reduce the number of plant workers by having IEs use industrial engineering methods to set personnel levels. This raised tensions between management and labor. When people retired in November, IEs performed job combinations rather than hiring replacement workers or recalling laid-off workers. This practice was made possible by a rule in the National Agreement, which stipulated that two retirees should be replaced by only one person.[7] Under normal circumstances, when one person quitted he or she was replaced by one person, but GM in the 2000s was under severe business pressure and had excess personnel, so management was pushed to gradually but forcibly reduced employee numbers based on the Secured Employment Levels (SEL) mechanism, part of which was the "every two retirees should be replaced by one person" rule.[8]

In Japan, the process for reducing man-hours varies depending on the firm. A target number of man-hours is set carefully by management after extensive planning. The target is then communicated to the workshop, where the head of the workshop involves the workers in working out a plan for meeting the target. Regarding this process, GM was not as well organized as Toyota.[9]

The actual situation of man-hour reductions at GM was as follows. First, the IE consults with the foreman. If the foreman says, for example, "the workload for this process is a bit light, I think we could add a little more work here," the IE returns to his office and drafts a man-hour reduction plan based on the foreman's opinion. Next, it is communicated to workers that the task(s) performed at a certain position in the assembly line will be transferred to a neighboring worker's position and integrated into the process that that worker performs. A worker whose workload is increased in this way complains to his or her local union shop steward, and a grievance is filed, increasing tensions between labor and management. In cases such as this, the worker whose work has increased may truly be unable to do their job well, or they may simply be complaining. In any case, at the Detroit Big Three, man-hours were reduced unilaterally by engineers and foremen without consulting workers.

When we interviewed UAW officials about this kind of labor–management relationship, they answered that the union wants to change the traditional structure of top-down management. They suggested that things would be different if workers were consulted in advance. For example, if an IE were to say to workers, "I am considering this man-hour reduction proposal, but do you have any other suggestions?" many disputes, which are common and take up much time and effort, could be eliminated.

A major goal of factory management is to improve productivity and quality. At Plant A numerical targets were set loosely through labor–management negotiations. For example, quality was expressed in terms of cost, as the yield rate of non-defective products. The numerical indicators at Plant A were summarized in a "scorecard." Operation rate was represented by the item "schedule attainment to plan" within the larger item of "responsiveness."

In an automobile factory, the assembly line is very long, so breakdowns and malfunctions often occur at some point in the production process, causing the entire line to stop. For this reason, it is almost impossible for an auto plant to have an operation rate, or "machine up time," of 100%. For example, if an assembly line is operated for 10 hours a day and during that time the line is down for one hour, the operation rate is 90%. During the hour of "machine down time," thousands of production workers in the plant have nothing to do, but they still get paid. This is a waste for the company, so factory management is always trying to improve the operation rate. An operation rate of 100% means that the productivity target has been achieved. If the operation rate exceeds 100%, this means that the initial target was too low or that the PDCA (plan-do-check-act) cycle is sloppy. How can the operation rate exceed 100%? As line stops are inevitable, target operation rates assume a certain amount of machine down time. So if the actual down time is less than assumed, the operation rate will exceed 100%. Consider, for example, an individual process for which the cycle time is set at 60 seconds. These 60 seconds might include an assumed line stoppage time of 4 seconds due to someone pulling the andon cord, plus an additional assumed stoppage time of 2 seconds due to mechanical failure. In such a case, the expected time of actual work to complete the process is 54 seconds per unit. This means that if there are no stoppages and the process is completed in 54 seconds, the operation rate would be over 110% on the scorecard.

Furthermore, because overtime work to meet production targets was included in target operation rates, the assembly line was set to run at a faster speed than the production plan would require. For example, in the case of a production plan of 60 units per hour, the line speed might be actually set to 63 units per hour. One might wonder why the union did not oppose this practice as a case of work intensification. The reason is interesting. In the body department, for example, 70 units per hour were produced, and production continued during lunch break to accumulate inventory. The union did not object to this, because if eight hours' worth of production could be finished in six and a half hours, workers could finish their work before their clock-out time, and then sit around at the plant until it is time to go home. This kind of practice was the outcome of negotiations between labor and management.

If there was a one-hour delay because of a line stoppage, the foreman asked the workers to work through their lunch break and skip their afternoon break. The lunch and afternoon breaks were 50 minutes in total. In return for doing this, the foreman offered to pay the production workers a 50% premium wage rate. They agreed because they had already taken an hour break during the line stoppage, and they could receive a pay premium. This kind of work practice was possible in Detroit because the production process was designed in a way that allows a large amount of inventory to be produced and held, even in the middle of the assembly process. It could never happen in Japan because inventory is considered a form of wastefulness and kept to a bare minimum.

When management did not accurately grasp the number of employees at their plants, and when operation rates did not play a role as accurate performance indicators, negotiations between labor and management over the number of personnel continued endlessly and resulted in situations like those described above. These problems could be called a "failure of management" in a sense. It appeared on paper that the number of personnel had decreased at the end of the year, but it had not decreased in practice. Owing to the lack of rigor in management, there was room for ambiguity and deception in negotiations between labor and management. These problematic practices were common at the old Plant A, which closed in 2006; it is said that in the new Plant A, which opened the same year, efforts are being made to overcome them.

Division of labor and quality control in the United States

The strict division of labor is a "character trait" of American management. Owing to this, productivity control and quality control have traditionally been thoroughly specialized. One manifestation of this is that in US auto plants the inspector in the final process is in charge of quality control. General workers who are not inspectors have nothing to do with inspection work because it is beyond the scope of their jobs. Of course, inspectors are ultimately responsible for quality control in Japan as well, but in Japanese auto plants general production workers are also responsible for quality to some degree, as part of their "irregular" work.

In the 1970s, poor quality was a major problem at US auto plants. When inspectors in the final process of the assembly line found defects, they relayed this information to engineers; the production workers were not involved in the process. Engineers would then go to the shop floor to tell workers what to do, but they showed no interest in questions or suggestions from workers. The atmosphere in the workshop was such that workers tended not to ask engineers questions; when they did, discussions did not go well or produce good outcomes. Engineers did not like any infringement on their authority, and their attitude was authoritarian.

Statistical process control (SPC)

In 1985, a new position was established at Plant A, called statistical process control (SPC). This position was occupied by union members rather than specialist engineers. Applicants were required to learn the basics of quality control and statistics.

After this position was created, engineers began to listen to SPC workers, whose job was to collect data on poor quality in the workshop, and to consult with them on specific issues. SPC-engineer cooperation worked best in the paint department, followed by the body department, but it went less well in the assembly department.

When the SPC role was first established, it was not well developed. For example, in the paint department, if a defect was found (such as dirt in a paint job), an engineer was contacted, the defect was fixed, and that was the end of it. The real value of the SPC came about only later, when SPC workers not only contacted the engineers but also discussed with them measures to prevent the defect from occurring in the future. In this way, the data collected was used to address the source of quality control issues, and the results were reflected in the standardized work table.

The plant quality council

The SPC role was an attempt to reduce the gap between production workers and engineers in the workshop. The "plant quality council," on the other hand, was an attempt to reduce the labor–management gap in the entire plant. This attempt can be regarded as the American pursuit of a labor–management consultation system like those that are widely practiced in Japan and Germany. The council is a place for discussion between labor and management on how they can cooperate on making progress toward meeting plant targets, at the plant level, in the body, paint, and assembly areas, and at the individual workshop level. An equal number of representatives from labor and management attend and discuss issues at each level. For example, when the highest plant-level quality council reports on the safety of the entire plant, discussions are carried out regarding the setting of, and measures for meeting, plant-level goals. At the area level, based on the plant-level goals, safety discussions are held in the body, paint, and assembly departments, and at the workshop level, consultations are held between the day and night shifts.

In terms of cooperation between labor and management, the plant quality council can be seen as a breakthrough for American auto plants, which have traditionally been characterized by adversarial labor–management relations. However, the effectiveness of the council was uneven. When a plant manager who understood the quality council was in charge, its processes were performed diligently and with positive results. But in other cases the council did not meet or meets only irregularly, or the atmosphere was hostile. For example, an attendee from the union side might point out problems in the operations of an attendee from the management side, leading the management attendee to be reprimanded by his boss on the spot. When interactions like this occurred frequently, the quality council itself gradually became less open and loses its meaning.

In both production efficiency and quality control, the methods of Japanese automobile manufacturers have been applied at Plant A since the 1990s. A different "quality meeting" group apart from the plant quality council was also established, but in the 2000s, due to deteriorating labor–management relations, the union ceased sending representatives to this meeting. As a result, the meeting became management-only, consisting of a customer satisfaction manager, the plant manager, and three area managers.

New inspection processes

Quality inspection at the shop floor level at Plant A has changed in several ways. In the 1990s, a new inspection system called *verification stations* was introduced to supplement the final inspection at the end of the production process (see Figure 4.3). At seven points in the assembly process and at one point each in body and paint operations, verification stations were established to check the quality of a vehicle in the process of being produced. Similar in-progress quality checking is the norm in Japanese auto plants.

In the case of the assembly department, the reason for these midway checks is clear: if a defect is identified before the vehicle reaches the end of the assembly line, it is no longer necessary to disassemble and reassemble the vehicle in order to fix it. In the body department, the verification station is set up at the end of the process. Here, metal finishers inspect the body, check all welds, and repair any defects.

Another important change to the traditional inspection process was that, with the introduction of verification stations, inspections were carried out by highly trained inspection professionals who could assess and control quality more accurately. Previously, inspecting in the body department had been done by metal finishers who were union members. These "inspectors" could not be trusted to do a reliable job; if the production workshop was trying to achieve a certain production volume, the foreman could ask them to loosen quality standards, and they would comply because they were colleagues of the body department workers. Similarly, in the paint department, if dirt was found on the paint, the inspector, who was friends with paint department workers, sometimes said there was no problem in order to help

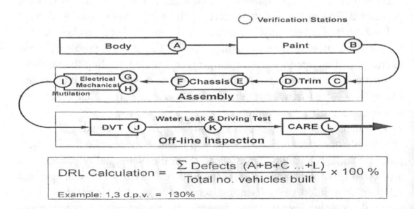

Figure 4.3 Quality control: Verification stations (Source: UAW Internal Document).

achieve the production volume needed to keep the assembly line running. Ideally, in the case of the assembly process, the person inspecting at the verification station should be a union member, and job rotation should be carried out so that all workers learn the inspection process. This has not happened at GM, however.

Along with the verification stations, a quality control feature called the *blue card* was introduced in the 1990s. This card is essentially a checklist for defects. Blue cards are usually written at one of two locations: the final inspection of the final process in which the defect is found or the verification station that identifies the defect. Normally, when a verification station worker finds a defect, they contact their foreman, who fills out a blue card. If a defect is found in the final process, the auditor himself fills out a blue card. In both cases, the blue cards are sent to the foreman at the workshop where the defect occurred.

A foreman who receives a blue card is supposed to go to the workshop and talk to the team coordinator to deal with the problem. At the workshop, immediate measures are taken to fix the defect, and then the root cause of the problem is investigated and measures are taken to prevent its recurrence. Typically, a transcribed blue card is reported by the foreman at a quality meeting within 24 hours. Quality meetings are held daily for such reports.

Finally, *teamwork* is encouraged, not only for "unskilled" production workers but also for skilled workers such as electricians, machinists, and pipefitters. This effort is intended to remove the negative effects of skilled workers' "territoriality." Previously, skilled workers stayed at their cribs, organized by the skilled trades. The cribs were packed with parts and tools, and some were quite messy. Some were even reported to contain beds.[10] When skilled workers went to the site of a line breakdown, they then had to return to their cribs to fetch the parts and tools needed to make repairs. Because the plant was large and the cribs were located at one end, the time loss due to these round trips was significant. During that time the line remained stopped, and production workers were being paid for doing nothing.

Teamwork was introduced to eliminate the wastefulness generated by skilled trade employees' work methods. Although the process still has room for improvement, various measures have been put in place to reduce the time it takes for skilled workers to get parts, such as establishing teams, assigning responsibilities to each team, and storing parts at the center of the plant.

As this chapter has shown, US auto plants have been struggling to reform their production sites, especially leading up to and following GM's 2009 bankruptcy. The first task has been to address "top-down management," "vertical organizational division," "job territoriality," and other aspects of traditional American mass production plants. GM plants have continued to work on various reforms, including improving employee motivation and communication within the organization in an attempt to dramatically reduce the number of job types and broaden the scope of seniority rights. However, as we will see in Chapter 5, their journey of reform is still under way.

Notes

1　The content of this chapter is based on Ishida and Shinohara (2010) and Shinohara (2014), as well as records of interviews conducted with UAW officers and others during September 11–24, 2005, and on April 1, May 6, June 17, and August 17, 2016.
2　For details, see Shinohara (2003).
3　Bergglen (1998).
4　Krafcik (1986).
5　In Japan, the laying off of full-time workers is often prevented by the use of relocations and various other methods even when job combinations are carried out. However, the UAW has no choice but to oppose job combinations because they threaten the maintenance of employment for union members.
6　The Jobs Bank was a program introduced following the 1984 National Agreement negotiations by which laid-off workers received subsidy payments from GM after their unemployment benefits ran out. This program was discontinued with GM's 2009 bankruptcy. See Ishida and Shinohara (2010), Chapter 8, for details.
7　Ishida and Shinohara (2010), chapter 7.
8　*Ibid.*, chapter 8.
9　*Ibid.*, chapter 7.
10　Record of interviews with UAW officers and others conducted in September 2005.

References

Berggren C. (1998). *The Volvo Experience: Alternatives to Lean Production in the Swedish Auto Industry*. Basingstoke: MacMillan.
Krafcik, John. (1986). *Learning From NUMMI*, IMVP-MIT, Internal Working Paper, September.
Ishida, Mitsuo, and Kenichi Shinohara. (2010). *GM no Keiken*. Tokyo: Chuo Keizaisha.
Shinohara, Kenichi. (2003). *Tenkanki no Amerika Roushikankei*. Kyoto: Minerva Shobo.
Shinohara, Kenichi. (2014). *Amerika Jidosha Sangyo*. Tokyo: Chuo Koron Shinsha.

5 GM's Global Manufacturing System (GMS) and the Union

The link between reform and improvement in productivity and quality

This chapter examines the relationship between General Motors' Global Manufacturing System, or GMS, and the UAW. Launched in 1996, GMS is an integrated production system that has been deployed not only in GM's American plants but in suppliers and all GM plants around the world.

Following the global financial crisis in 2008, GM declared Chapter 11 bankruptcy on June 1, 2009, during the first six months of the Obama administration. Management restructuring during the bankruptcy period required reforms in various aspects of company operations. Some reforms were accomplished in a relatively short period of time by top management decision. These included decisions regarding specific brands and models, review of alliances, moving production to different sites, and review of product and international strategies. Other reforms, however, such as those involving GMS, could not be carried out in the short term because they involve changes in the way the production workplace is organized and operated and are heavily dependent on the cooperation and performance of production workers. Professor Takahiro Fujimoto refers to this kind of reform as "international competition in capability building" and "deep competitiveness."[1] Reforms of this kind have not progressed steadily due to labor–management conflict in the workplace, which can best be understood through field surveys.

In order to understand reforms aimed at improving productivity and quality at production sites, it is necessary to clarify the specific linkages between reforms and productivity and quality improvements. Until now, however, researchers in the United States have not gone much further than using the keyword "team concept" to describe these organizational reforms. Against the background of the traditional rigid and fragmented seniority-based job classification of the US auto industry, researchers

DOI: 10.4324/9781003282426-5

appear to have been strongly attracted to the more flexible working image associated with small groups or teams. But they have failed, for the most part, to identify and describe the concrete links between core reforms and productivity and quality.

Ishida and Shinohara (2010) clarified to a considerable degree the specific linkages between reform and productivity/quality improvements at GM up to the time of their 2005 survey. However, the deeper reforms that GM was forced to undertake in the wake of its 2009 bankruptcy, under Chapter 11 of the US Bankruptcy Code, have not yet been adequately studied, particularly with regard to their links with productivity and quality improvement. In this chapter we examine what has been learned up to now.[2]

A case study of Ford

Ford has a production system similar to GMS, which Cutcher-Gershenfeld et al. describe in their book *Inside the Ford–UAW Transformation: Pivotal Events in Valuing Work and Delivering Results* (The MIT Press, 2015). Before examining GM's GMS, let us consider the Ford case study.

According to Cutcher-Gershenfeld et al., Ford was the first US auto company to discuss a teamwork agreement in the mid-1980s. Production workers at Ford have become involved in production planning, quality control, inventory control, and workplace staffing, which were formerly white-collar jobs. The goal of this change was to increase efficiency within work teams and thereby increase productivity across entire plants. This was an extension of the concept presented by Cutcher-Gershenfeld et al. in their 1998 book *Knowledge Driven Work*, and it pioneered Ford's company-wide Continuous Improvement Work Group (CIWG) initiative.

In the first 30 years after "continuous improvement" (kaizen) came to the attention of US automakers, nothing covering continuous improvement activities like the CIWG appeared in Ford's National Agreement. During this time, the way continuous improvement was dealt with was left up to the managers of each plant. Continuous improvement was negotiated in the National Agreement for the first time in 2011. Compared to GM, which has been working on this kind of reform on a nationwide level since the early 2000s, Ford's response was delayed by about ten years.

Based on language in the 2003 National Agreement, UAW executives visited the Ford plants in Europe (the Valencia plant in Spain and the Cologne plant in Germany), where implementation of the Ford Production System, which included some kaizen activities, was more advanced than in the United States. What they learned there helped pave the way for the introduction of kaizen in Ford's American plants. In the actual operation of improvement activities, top-down leadership and plant-wide deployment and planning were discussed. Eliminating disparities among plants in the progress of organizational reform was also a top priority for Ford. Against this background, management and the union tackled specific kaizen activities stipulated in the National Agreement from 2011 onward. The following description of this process is based on Cutcher-Gershenfeld et al.[3]

To begin with, the National Continuous Improvement Forum was formed to oversee the overall control system. Its members are the Vice President in charge of manufacturing, the Vice President in charge of labor affairs, the General Manager in charge of labor affairs, and the Director of union relations from the company side, and the Vice President of the National Ford Council and a UAW Administrative Assistant from the union side. The forum is ultimately responsible for the transfer of work teams and the Joint Continuous Improvement Charter.

The National Continuous Improvement Forum's Mission Statement reads as follows:

> The joint parties are committed to implementing work groups/teams to a consistent standard supporting the global manufacturing strategy as defined in Appendix J. Our beliefs and behaviors must honor standardization and continuous improvement to enable our work groups/teams to deliver "One Manufacturing – Best in the World."[4]

Its Guiding Principle is:

> The parties pledge to work together on continuous improvement initiatives at every organizational level to improve quality, operating efficiency including plant cost performance, work relationships, work group/team effectiveness, job security, and quality of work life.[5]

This management by objectives for the entire organization is broken down into "large goals," "mid-range goals," and "small goals." Targets are set for the following eight processes within a plant:

1) Aligned and Capable Organization: Working Group and Team Structure
2) Standard Team Leader Roles and Responsibility
3) Standardized Team Leader Selection and De-Selection Process
4) Team Leader Training
5) Manufacturing Work Group Technical Skills Competency Training
6) Working Group / Team Implementation Plan
7) Existing Team Leader Transition Plan
8) Charter Change Management Process

Collective bargaining is used as a forum for codifying the scope of labor agreements and the practice of work team groups. Work groups, team composition, and team leaders are described in the agreement as follows.

Work Team/Group Structure: manufacturing facilities will have any combination of the following teams/groups.

- *Production Work Group*: comprises approximately 20–30 non-skilled trades workers and team leaders on an assembly line.
- *Manufacturing Work Group*: approximately 10–20 unskilled, semi-skilled, and skilled trade employees with a team leader (Production or Skilled Trades) working with no traditional lines of demarcation and operating and maintaining equipment within capabilities.
- *Mechanical Work Team*: all Skilled Trades teams with a Skilled Trades Team Leader working within their capabilities with no traditional lines of demarcation.

Team leaders: both labor and management will spend time discussing the roles and responsibilities of team leaders, selection processes, training, and compensation for the following four items.

1) *Plant Governance*: The Local Continuous Improvement Forum (LCIF), which consists of the Plant Manager, HR Manager, Plant UAW Chairman, UAW Bargaining Representatives, have responsibility for process oversight.
2) *Leader Selection Process*: Candidates are scored using a standard set of questions including experience and versatility (25 pts), SQDCPME (Safety, Quality, Delivery, Cost, People, Maintenance, and Environment) knowledge and work habits (40 pts), and people/leadership skills (35 pts). Interviews and final selection are made by the Superintendent, Team Manager (First Line Supervisor), and designated UAW Bargaining Representative.
3) *Competency Training*: The parties agreed to jointly develop a training curriculum to support standardization and continuous improvement. Existing and newly assigned team leaders will participate in the training.
4) *Compensation for Team Leaders*: Newly assigned team leaders receive an incremental $1.50 and existing team leaders receive $8.55 over their existing hourly rate of pay.

Cutcher-Gershenfeld et al. explain that the additional $8.55 received by the team leaders is more than team leaders receive at GM or Chrysler. This is a reflection of Ford's high expectations for team leaders' contributions.

According to these authors, no concrete progress was made concerning teamwork during the 2011 National Agreement negotiations at Ford, but it is significant that, for the first time, the agreement defines the work group/team structure to some degree.

Significant reform finally took place at Ford in 2011, 15 years after the reform of the Ford Production System began in the late 1990s. The reason for the delay was that neither the UAW nor the company was positive about the joint labor–management plan. The company was concerned about the erosion of its traditional managerial rights, and the UAW was reluctant to make fundamental changes in the way work was carried out. However, the 2011 agreement finally led both labor and management to prioritize "knowledge-driven" aspects of workplace operations.

Detroit's Big Three have often regarded the Japanese automobile factory, and especially the Toyota production system, as a benchmark. However, their efforts have not always achieved desired outcomes due to (1) the failure of performance management based on continuous improvement activities to function effectively and (2) the inability to introduce a merit pay system for production workers. Next we turn to GM, in order to clarify the mechanisms GM put in place to try to improve productivity and quality at the shop floor level.

GMS and related reforms at GM Plant A

GM's Plant A is located in Michigan and has around 3,000 employees. It began operations in 1935 and moved to its current location in 2006. The plant produces popular CUV (crossover-utility vehicle) models. (The difference between a CUV and an SUV, or sports utility vehicle, is that an SUV uses a truck chassis while a CUV uses a car chassis.)

In the new plant, work organization reform which was impossible in the past has been made through a process of repeated trial-and-error. Following the attempts to "humanize" labor that began in the 1970s under the banner QWL (Quality of Work Life), the focus gradually turned to "refining and concretely implementing policy management," especially in the 2000s.

Policy management refers to activities that efficiently execute medium- and long-term management plans and short-term management policies. These are carried out in accordance with the management cycle of "Plan → Do → Check → Act" (the PDCA cycle). Management believed that there was considerable room for improvement at the shop floor level.

Table 5.3 shows the labor–management consultation system created after the labor–management negotiations in the autumn of 2015. Through this system, labor and management are jointly involved in policy management and business plan deployment.

Three major areas of reform, described below, involve GMS, verification stations, and core teams.

GMS

General Motors has applied its GMS production system framework not only to its US plants but also to its global plants in Mexico, Brazil, China, South Korea (Daewoo), Great Britain (Vauxhall), Germany, Poland, and Spain (Opel).

GM's plants are ranked according to the level of built-in-quality (BIQ) of their production site systems. BIQ Level 5 is the highest level. As of 2016, no plants had reached this level. Most plants were ranked at levels 2 or 3. Several around the world were ranked at Level 4, including Plant A. Plants with high rankings often receive production quotas for popular vehicles and incentives for further investment. Conversely, plants with low rankings risk facing closure. GM headquarters uses this ranking system to motivate plant managers and push reforms.

Figure 5.1 presents a conceptual diagram of the criteria (requirements) for achieving BIQ Level 3. The basic criteria consist of 44 items, called "Level III Absolutes": 16 items for built-in-quality, 10 for employee involvement, 4 for standardization, 6 for lead time reduction, and 8 for kaizen (continuous improvement). A plant that meets these basic requirements must then go through the additional procedures to obtain Level 3 certification.

Table 5.1 provides a summary of the Quality Control Metrics for BIQ Level 3.

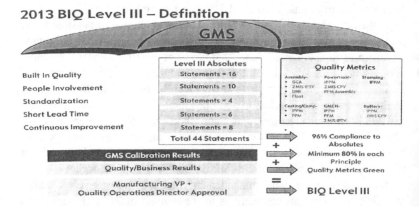

Figure 5.1 Conceptual diagram of the basic criteria for BIQ Level 3 certification under GMS (Source: UAW–GM Internal Document).

Table 5.1 Overview of Quality Control Metrics at BIQ Level 3

BIQ Level 3 Metrics- Vehicle Assembly		
Metric/Requirement	**Target**	**Detail/Comments**
GMS/BIQ Absolutes	≥ %	44 total absolutes.
DRR	≥ %	All-in Plant average for current + 3 prior months
Repair Float	min	Global Shop Directors (Lead by) have defined common method to measure – Plant average for current + 3 prior months
2 MIS IPTV Warranty	3MMA ≤ MY Glidepath	Volume weighted target by plant. (Must remain within %). Plant average for current + 3 prior months meets glide path.
GCA	Glidepath	Model target(s) for current + 3 prior months meets glide path
Decertification	All	External Cal Abs < ; Repair Float, GCA, 2MIS NOK for 3 consecutive months. *Require 6 month window at minimum before application of recertification.*

Source: UAW–GM Internal Document; specific figures and names redacted by the author.

Table 5.2 Built-in-quality Level III Absolutes

BIQ 1	PQS Developed & Common
BIQ 2	PQS Communicated & Understood
BIQ 3	PFMEA Risk Reduction & Annual Review
BIQ 6	Change Control Process & Product Validation
BIQ 7	Change Control PTR
BIQ 9	Process Control Plans Implemented
BIQ 14	Error Proofing Validation
BIQ 16	Verification Stations / CARE
BIQ 17	Effective Quality Checks
BIQ 18	Alarm & Escalation
BIQ 21	Non-Conforming Material
BIQ 23	In Process measures
BIQ 24	Feed back / Feed Forward
BIQ 25	Fast Response (5F)
BIQ 27	Quality Resource Plan
BIQ 28	Strategic Quality Plan
BIQ Level III Built In Quality TOTAL 16 Absolutes	

Source: GM Internal Document.

Table 5.2 shows 16 of the BIQ "Level III Absolutes." These are part of a set of indicators that production workers are involved with. These specific indicators correspond to "small targets" in the "large targets → medium targets → small targets" management-by-objectives scheme used at Plant A. To understand the work organization changes and how they affect production workers, it is necessary to compare the actual conditions of production work against the "small target" indexes. Implementation of this mechanism, which was refined through negotiations for the 2015 National Agreement, has only just begun and remains an issue for the future.

As explained above, since 2000 GMS has been systematically broken down into detailed management items and divided into five built-in-quality levels with accompanying benchmarks. However, the critical question is: Is this system working well? Even if the system is rational, to operate it successfully requires cooperation from and coordination among production workers, engineers, and managers. In the end, it is the workers who must operate just-in-time production, continuous improvement, and other Japanese-inspired work methods. Management has to negotiate with production workers and their union to gain their cooperation. Therefore, examining and understanding the realities of management–union negotiations on these issues is important.

Verification stations

Quality has become a more serious focus of policy management in the 2000s. Traditionally, automobile factories in the United States conducted integrated quality inspections only at the end of the production process. Now, as Figure 5.2 shows, which overlaps with Figure 4.3 in Chapter 4, verification stations have been added at various points in the production process. In the example shown, there is one each in the Body and Paint departments, seven during assembly, and three more in the final off-line inspection.

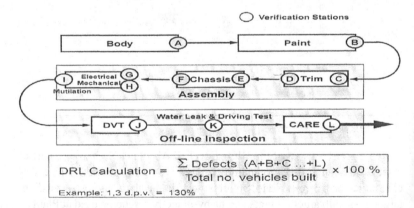

Figure 5.2 Multiple verification stations added to the quality control process (Source: UAW Internal Document).

A major feature of this process is that it is direct production workers (those with high seniority) who perform the quality checks at the verification stations. Under the previous system, a specialized quality department carried out quality checks at the end of the final assembly line. The change to the present system was part of an effort to reverse excessive division of labor by expanding the scope of jobs performed by production and skilled trades workers.

Core teams

Core teams at Plant A were created by combining the specialized Problem Solver position and the Product Development team (PDT), which were created in the 1990s. Core teams function mainly as continuous improvement specialists. They play a particularly active role when there is a model change or when a new vehicle is launched. Since GM's bankruptcy, management has collaborated more closely with suppliers, especially on quality issues, and core teams visit suppliers to resolve issues.[6]

In the past, with regard to policy management, there was sometimes insufficient communication and ambiguous division of responsibilities among plant organizational units due to excessive division of labor. As a result, the implementation of policy management was often inconsistent or incoherent. Even if production workers were directly instructed to practice continuous improvement methods, it was difficult for them to identify targets for improvement such as "unreasonableness, inconsistency, or waste." This is why GM introduced core teams, which correspond to the kaizen teams that specialize in problem-solving and continuous improvement at Toyota plants in Japan. Core teams carry out continuous improvement functions that production workers alone cannot perform and facilitate communication between management levels in the plant and with suppliers.

Especially since the bankruptcy of 2009, the roles of GMS, verification stations, and core teams have been strengthened, and precise policy management has made significant progress in GM plants. As a result, GM's development of a production system along the lines of that seen at Toyota has advanced, but since the actual operation has only just started, further observation is required to evaluate its effectiveness.

Although the Toyota production system serves as a kind of guideline or benchmark, the strong path dependency of American labor–management relations creates unique challenges for work organization in the areas of (1) labor–management consultation and cooperation, (2) broad-banding of wage systems, and (3) the difficulty of internal promotion for production workers. As will be described below, even if work organization is transformed into a form more suitable for policy management, these challenges remain.

Remaining challenges

Labor–management consultation

Needless to say, carrying out policy management requires cooperation at the shop floor level. In the case of automobile production, as Fujimoto argues, manufacturing is based on integral architecture, where the production process is complex and highly refined. Work organization reform cannot be effectively carried out by merely using top-down decision-making. In this context, American automakers introduced a kind of labor–management consultation system in the 1990s. Table 5.3 shows the labor–management consultation system compiled after the labor–management negotiations in the autumn of 2015, following some twists and turns. This represented a major step forward given the history of adversarial labor–management relations in the US auto industry.

As can be seen from Table 5.3, councils were established at three levels: upper, middle, and lower. The top UAW–GM Leadership Council holds discussions among the top decision-makers (the UAW and GM headquarters) of labor and management. The middle UAW–GM Operations Council functions at the international level for the union and at the corporate level for GM, and the working-level UAW–GM Local Leadership Council operates at the plant level. Although a labor–management consultation system started in the 1990s, at that time it only operated on a regular basis at the local level. It was not until 2015 that a formal central top-level consultation mechanism between labor and management was established. Since 2015, with the new UAW–GM council structure, disparities among plants in GMS implementation and other areas have been reduced.

Prior to 2015, the labor–management consultation system only operated at the local level, and it was extremely unstable due to wide variations in understanding and support among the plant managers appointed by GM headquarters every few years. If a plant manager was appointed who had a positive attitude toward labor–management collaboration, the system ran smoothly, but if a plant manager was appointed who had little understanding of the consultation system, it was ineffective or suspended. Therefore, GM's adoption in 2015 of a more systematic approach, including labor–management consultation at the middle and upper levels of the company and the union, was an important step forward in terms of the ability to introduce coherent company-wide policy management based on labor–management collaboration. This new labor–management consultation system has just begun, and it is hoped that its actual operation will be the subject of research in the future.

The incentives for plant managers differ greatly between the United States and Japan. In the case of a plant manager in Japan, reducing costs through continuous improvement activities extending to the whole plant is a central goal and a critical yardstick by which the plant manager's performance is

Table 5.3 New UAW–GM council structure (2015–)

Name	Chair 1	Chair 2	Frequency	Purpose 1	Purpose 2	Purpose 3	Purpose 4	Attendance
UAW–GM Leadership Council	Vice President	Director of UAW	Quarterly	Overall direction for implementation of GMS	A forum for information sharing regarding competitive benchmarking and global revision of GMS	Review BPD (Business Plan Development) in order to evaluate progress of the plan and support implementation measures	Resolve Product Quality Resolution Process conflicts and concerns	Designated by chair
UAW–GM Operations Council	Manufacturing Manager	UAW Int'l Servicing Rep.		Support for GMS implementation	Review progress of departmental activities such as Suggestions, VPAC, etc.	Review BPD in order to evaluate progress of the plan and support implementation measures	Resolve Product Quality Resolution Process conflicts and concerns	Designated by UAW–GM GMS Steering Committee
UAW–GM Local Leadership Council	Plant Manager	UAW Shop Committee Chairman	Monthly	Acts as the local steering committee for GMS implementation; provides support for the Core Teams	Review progress of departmental activities such as Suggestions, VPAC, etc.	Review BPD in order to evaluate progress of the plan and support implementation measures	Resolve Product Quality Resolution Process conflicts and concerns	1) President of Local Union; 2) Shop committee members; 3) Plant Manager's staff; 4) Personnel Director; 5) UAW Int'l Regional Rep. 6) Other members may be designated as appropriate.

Created by the author based on UAW internal documents and interviews with UAW officials.

evaluated. GM plant managers are also expected to reduce costs through continuous improvement activities in their plants, but the incentives to do so, for both production workers and managers, are insufficient to produce the kind of cost reductions seen at Toyota.

Thus, at GM, neither controls nor incentives are strong enough to encourage or force plant managers and other lower managers to aggressively pursue cost reduction based on continuous improvement. While greater emphasis has been placed on quality improvement in recent years, *production volume per se* remains the primary goal for plant managers and the primary criterion by which they are evaluated. It is true that systematic cost reduction is being emphasized more today than it was in the past, but in comparison with Toyota, the ability to achieve cost reductions remains weak.

Figure 5.3 summarizes the changes in policy focus on labor and management from the 1970s to today.

Table 5.4 summarizes the changes in the influence of different functions and positions within the plant organization over the past 20 years or so.

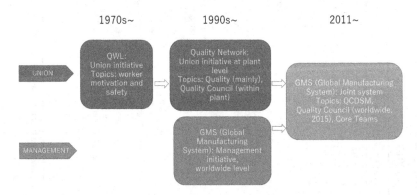

Figure 5.3 Policy focus of union and management (Source: created by the author).

Table 5.4 Changes in the influence of different functions and positions

Function or position	Change in influence
Engineer	Same or slightly decreased
Supervisor	Decreased
Quality department	Increased
Production worker	Slightly increased
CORE team	Started
Union appointee	Role: same; Number: reduced
Team leader	Increased

Created by the author, based on interviews with GM personnel.

The wage system

As a result of negotiations between labor and management in 2015, the hourly wage rate for direct production workers at Plant A is $29.07 per hour. There is no performance appraisal at present, and there are no prospects for the introduction of one in the future. As mentioned above, there were once 200 job classifications within Plant A and a corresponding number of wage rates. Since the 1990s, however, job classifications have been unified, so that the majority of production workers are paid the same wage rate. Temporary and newly hired workers receive lower wages.

Being promoted to the position of team leader, responsible for coordinating work on the shop floor, is the only possible promotion for a production worker. When a worker is promoted to team leader, his or her hourly wage is only increased by $1. Before the 2015 negotiations, the wage increase for team leaders was only $0.50. As noted earlier, employees at Ford receive an additional $8.55 per hour when they are promoted from production worker to team leader. As will be described below, in principle there is no promotion from team leader to higher positions at GM's Plant A.

The impact of the lack of performance reviews for production workers remains significant. As already noted, cooperation among workers is essential for successful policy management. However, in the absence of a performance evaluation system, there is a limit to how much general production workers will engage in "non-routine work" and how strongly they can be motivated to make improvements. As it is impossible to establish an individual performance evaluation system, profit-sharing plans have been introduced at Plant A that are tied to the number of units produced and to quality indices.[7]

Internal promotion for production workers

Like a performance-appraisal wage system, a smooth internal promotion system is desirable as a motivation for on-site production workers to engage in "non-routine work." Except for promotion to team leader, however, it is virtually impossible for a production worker to be promoted to a higher position. Promotions to team leader are determined by vacancies, seniority, and examination by the above-mentioned local leadership council.

It should be noted that not all workers desire to be promoted to the team leader position, as the financial incentive is small: a $1 per hour wage increase (compared to $8.55 at Ford). The main reason workers seek promotion to team leader is that it allows them to get out of full-time "on-line" assembly work, which is not only monotonous but also physically and mentally demanding, as it must be done at the line-speed set by management.

Promotion to team leader means moving from "on-line work" to "off-line work," where a person can work at his or her own pace.

For production workers at Toyota, in contrast to GM, it is possible to be promoted to managerial level positions and even to plant manager. In Japan, strict goals and roles are set for both production workers and managers using systematic plant policy management. Assessments are made of whether or not these goals are accomplished every fiscal year, and outstanding employees are promoted over the long term. In other words, Japan's rigorous PDCA cycles are closely matched with control and incentive systems and run relatively well. GM has its systematic GMS and labor–management consultation system, but the actual operation of these is not as smooth, stable, or refined as at Toyota.

Summary

The following are notable points from existing studies and surveys at GM:

1) Reduction of the number of job classifications to unified wage rates and expansion of the scope of seniority rights
2) Systematic improvement of the GMS framework
3) Introduction of new systems such as verification stations and core teams
4) Establishment of a company-wide labor–management consultation system
5) Individual evaluation (merit system) and internal promotion impossible for production workers

Since the 1990s, item 1 of the above list—the introduction of a unified wage rate system for a smaller number of job classifications and expansion of the scope of seniority rights—has progressed. Work on items 2, 3, and 4 began in the early 2000s and accelerated due to GM's bankruptcy in 2009. Achieving item 5, however, has proven to be impossible, and no progress has been made.

Broadly speaking, GM has succeeded in creating a "mechanism" for organization reform (i.e., it has strengthened policy management) for items 1 to 4. In particular, following bankruptcy in 2009, the pursuit of policy management using Toyota's work organization as a benchmark has been formally strengthened. However, motivation and control mechanisms necessary for implementing it remain weak.

At the time of our most recent survey in August of 2016, there were clearly some operational issues: the PDCA cycles were not yet functioning effectively. After the 2015 contract negotiations, the mechanisms for policy management were improved considerably compared to before, and could be said to be closer to the work organization system of Toyota, which is the benchmark. GM aims to incorporate key elements of Toyota's work organization system into its own, through GMS and the labor–management consultation system, which resemble those of Toyota. Conducting performance evaluation of union members and promoting production workers to any position above team leader remain impossible. Continued investigation in the future will be needed to evaluate how much progress GM makes in implementing the various organization reforms described above.

Addendum: Impact of the shift to EVs (electric vehicles) on work organizations

So far in this chapter, we have discussed GMS and labor–management relations. Finally, we will touch on the movement toward EVs.

Since the 2010s, there has been a rapid increase in global efforts to reduce dependence on oil and switch to clean energy technologies to tackle climate change. Furthermore, in August 2021, President Biden outlined a target of 50% EV sales share in 2030.[8] The EVs here include Battery Electric Vehicle (BEV), Fuel Cell Vehicle (FCV), and Plug-in Hybrid Vehicle (PHV).

The socio-economic prospects of EV adoption are still unpredictable in some respects.[9] However, the Detroit Three—GM, Stellantis, and Ford—are creating an environment that will produce EVs. In the case of GM, Chief Executive Officer Mary Barra said in 2018 that the company would proceed with restructuring across the board and at the same time spend $2.2 billion to completely renovate the Hamtramck plant, naming it the new Factory Zero, where it would build the GMC Hummer EV from 2022 and the Chevrolet Silverado EV, Cruise Origin, and other EVs from 2024.[10] This Factory Zero will employ more than 2,200 people at full capacity in the future. In addition, GM announced that the Orion Assembly Plant in Orion Township and the Spring Hill Assembly Plant in Tennessee will also be converted to electric vehicle production facilities.[11] At the same time, GM estimates that 80% of the assembly process for an EV is the same as that for conventional vehicles.[12]

On the other hand, the union's response on this issue in the 2019 National Agreement negotiations is as follows.

The UAW bargaining committee raised many concerns regarding the company's plans to increase its electric and autonomous vehicle lineup and expand the use of advanced processes. As a result, they said they won a commitment from the company to not only reaffirm that the introduction of new technology will not move work out of the bargaining unit but also ensure UAW members will be able to retain the higher-skilled work associated with new technology. Both parties agreed to establish a National Committee on Advanced Technology, made up of an equal number of union and management representatives. The committee will meet at least quarterly to discuss the impact of future technologies on UAW members and address instances where bargaining unit work has shifted out of the unit due to new manufacturing processes. The Plant New Technology Committee will be given access to information and participate in discussions with the national committee to work through issues at impacted locations.[13]

With the renovation of the former Hamtramck plant into Factory Zero, 435 of the former factory workers are still working on prototypes for new models in the renovated plant, 684 workers have been transferred to the Flint plant, Michigan, and Fort Wayne plant, Indiana, 130 workers have retired, and 140 workers have been laid off with recall rights.[14]

Once the plant is fully operational, more than 2,200 people will be employed at this Factory Zero, but as of October 2021, these Factory Zero workers have not yet been recalled to work. As of this writing, the new Local Agreements have not yet been made public, so the details of the situation at each factory are not known. We will have to wait and see what happens with these.

Notes

1 Fujimoto (2007), pp. 33–40.
2 Our thanks go to an official of UAW for his cooperation in an interview held on August 17, 2016, which provides the basis of much of this chapter. See also Shinohara (2014).
3 Cutcher-Gershenfeld et al. (2015), pp. 152–155.
4 UAW (2019a).
5 UAW (2019b).
6 Shinohara (2014), pp. 181–186.
7 UAW (2015), pp. 2–3.
8 The White House (2021).
9 International Energy Agency (2021).
10 General Motors (2021a).
11 General Motors (2020).
12 General Motors (2021b).
13 UAW (2019), p. 6.
14 Detroit Free Press (2021).

References

Cutcher-Gershenfeld, Joel, Dan Brooks, and Martin Mulloy. (2015). *Inside the Ford-UAW Transformation: Pivotal Events in Valuing Work and Delivering Results*. Cambridge: The MIT Press.

Cutcher-Gershenfeld, Joel et al.(1998). *Knowledge-Driven Work: Unexpected lessons from Japanese and United States work Practices*. Oxford: Oxford University Press.

Detroit Free Press. (2021). GM is Building Pre-Production Hummer EVs at Factory ZERO, Hiring to Follow, October 12th, 2021. Detroit Free Press. https://www.freep.com/story/money/cars/general-motors/2021/10/12/gm

-pre-production-hummer-evs-factory-zero-hiring/6095302001/. Accessed on January 19, 2022.

Fujimoto, Takahiro. (2007). *Competing to Be Really, Really Good.* Tokyo: International House of Japan.

General Motors. (2020). GM Investing $2 Billion to Transition Spring Hill, Tennessee Plant to Build Electric Vehicles, Including Cadillac LYRIQ, October 20th, 2020. General Motors. https://media.gm.com/media/us/en/gm/home.detail.html/content/Pages/news/us/en/2020/oct/1020-event.html. Accessed on January 19, 2022.

General Motors. (2021a, November 17). GM to Celebrate Grand Opening of Factory ZERO—An American EV Factory. General Motors. https://media.gm.com/media/us/en/gm/news.detail.html/content/Pages/news/us/en/2021/nov/1117-fz.html. Accessed on January 19, 2022.

General Motors. (2021b, November 18). GM Celebrates Grand Opening of Factory ZERO—An All EV Factory. General Motors. https://media.gm.com/media/me/en/gm/company.detail.html/content/Pages/news/me/en/2021/gm/11-18-GM-Celebrates-Grand-Opening-of-Factory-ZERO-an-all-EV-Factory.html. Accessed on January 19, 2022.

International Energy Agency. (2021). Prospects for Electric Vehicle Deployment. International Energy Agency. https://www.iea.org/reports/global-ev-outlook-2021/prospects-for-electric-vehicle-deployment. Accessed on January 18, 2022.

Ishida, Mitsuo. (2003). *Social Science of Work: Frontier of Labour Research.* Minerva Publishing Co., Ltd.

Ishida, Mitsuo, and Kenichi Shinohara. (2010). *GM's Experience: Lessons for Japan.* Chuo Keizai, Inc.

Ishida, Mitsuo, Yoshinori Tomita, and Naoki Mitani. (2009). *Job, Management, and Labor-Management Relations in the Japanese Automotive Industry: Organizational Management to Maintain Competitiveness, Chuo Keizai Sha.*

Rubinstein, Saul A., and T. A. Kochan. (2001). *Learning from Saturn: A Look at the Boldest Experiment in Corporate Governance and Employee Relations.* Ithaca: Cornell University Press.

Shinohara, Kenichi. (2014). *U.S. Automotive Industry: Field Reforms That Have Resumed Competitiveness.* Chuokoron Shinsha.

The White House. (2021, August 5). *Fact Sheet: President Biden Announces Steps to Drive American Leadership Forward on Clean Cars and Trucks.* https://www.whitehouse.gov/briefing-room/statements-releases/2021/08/05/fact-sheet-president-biden-announces-steps-to-drive-american-leadership-forward-on-clean-cars-and-trucks/. Accessed on January 18, 2022.

UAW. (2015, October). *UAW General Motors Contract Summary: Hourly Workers.*

UAW. (2019a). *Total Cost/Continuous Improvement.* UAW-Ford National Programs Center. https://www.uawford.org/ci. Accessed on January 18, 2022.

UAW. (2019b). *UAW General Motors Contract Summary.* UAW. https://uaw.org/wp-content/uploads/2019/10/56100-UAW_hourly-1.pdf. Accessed on January 18, 2022.

UAW Local 602 and GM Delta Township Plant. (2015). *2015 Agreement.*

6 Conclusion

Summary and overall analysis

This book has described an investigation of work organization reform in the US auto industry in terms of employment relations. Discussion of work organization reform increased in the United States in the 1980s, at which time the keyword "team concept" attracted attention and gained popularity as a prominent feature of the Japanese workplace. If workers were organized into autonomous teams and worked together cooperatively, the thinking went, workplace satisfaction, improved productivity, and better quality would follow. As we have explained in this book, we consider this view to be overly optimistic.

In the 1990s, the meaning of the term "team concept" became better understood, and its use subsided. Subsequently, a new term, "diversification," was used to explain the state of work organization reform in the United States. Job descriptions in Japanese companies are not as narrow as they are in the traditional American workplace, and the degree of worker autonomy is not necessarily strong. It gradually became recognized that management control systems in Japan are strict, and discussion of work organization reform increasingly took this into account.

While some previous research described Japanese work organization as being under strong management control, no US study researched or described the system of management control of the Japanese work organization in detail. The system of management control is intimately connected with the direct relationship between the shop floor and employment relations. The most important objectives are productivity and quality improvement indexes. Therefore, there was a need for the actual conditions and details of plant management control systems and employment relations to be explored.

Against this background, Rubinstein and Kochan described work organization reform efforts that were carried out at Saturn with the aim

DOI: 10.4324/9781003282426-6

of improving productivity and quality, focusing on four new units and working arrangements: self-directed work teams, problem-solving teams, labor–management joint committees, and module advisors (see Table 1.1). However, Rubinstein and Kochan were insufficiently aware of the aspect of performance management itself, so their analysis was weak and lacked detailed description.

Subsequent research by Cutcher-Gershenfeld et al. drew attention to the importance of "continuous improvement" activities and "knowledge-driven" work. However, these scholars describe these in parallel, neglecting to elucidate the important relationship between them. As we have explained in the preceding chapters of this book, our research shows that the performance management system regulates the continuous improvement process as well as the work allocation of line workers. It is vital that researchers and auto industry leaders understand the reality of labor–management relations, the importance of the "performance management" viewpoint, and the relationship between performance management and work realities in the US auto industry. In this book we have tried to clarify this, using survey and field research, in order to fill in the void left by other academic studies of work organization reform.

Chapter 2 discusses the historical context of a current job transfer and promotion rules and the seniority structure of the Detroit Big Three auto plants. Our primary sources were past National Agreements and arbitration records as well as interviews with company representatives and union officials.

The National Agreement contains broad, basic rules concerning work organization that at first glance appear to be quite clear, simple, and easy to understand. However, underlying the language of the National Agreement are many historical conflicts between labor and management. These conflicts are not at all obvious in the current wording and remain hidden from many readers. However, even a single word can have deep meaning with roots in the distant past. Without an understanding of this historical background and a familiarity with the actual production system inside the factory, there are many clauses in the National Agreement which are difficult for an outsider to understand. Such an understanding and familiarity are also necessary for understanding how traditional work organizations based on narrow job classifications and seniority present difficulties for the adoption of a team concept that requires the transfer and utilization of "flexible" workers. Therefore, Chapter 2 aims to:

1) Link the National Agreement with arbitration awards (something that has not previously been done)
2) Highlight critical elements of work organization in the Detroit Big Three, in particular, job transfer and promotion rules

3) Identify problems associated with current work organization, in particular the team concept

In discussing these three topics, various related points were raised in this chapter. We clarified employee transfer and promotion rules while describing the structure and historical development of seniority rights up to the current National Agreements. Over the course of the development of transfer and promotion rules, many labor–management conflicts occurred during contract negotiations and some were resolved through arbitration. The most important issues of conflict concerned how to deal with seniority rules, and job assignments within the same job classification, and secondary job openings. As the years passed, the scope of transfers and promotion was expanded and the use of seniority rights was strengthened; at the same time, the number of arbitration cases decreased.

Chapter 3 analyzes work organization reform at the plant level, focusing on GM's Plant A. Chapter 2 explained the structure and historical evolution of seniority and transfer/promotion rules, mainly based on the National Agreement and arbitration records, and the case study of Plant A in Chapter 3 illustrates how these played out in actual work organization reform up until 2009. The main three points can be summarized as follows:

1) The areas that are and are not subject to regulation in the work organization of Plant A are clarified. Job assignment changes, which were traditionally determined at the foreman's discretion, are now determined by seniority rights, something the local union pushed for many years. However, no rules are in place that cover the filling of secondary job openings, and this issue remains a point of discussion between labor and management.

2) In exchange for the new regulations on job assignment changes, plant management won union approval for the introduction of the team concept. At first, the union cooperated with the introduction of the team concept, which had been a major topic since the 1980s, with the expectation that it would make the workplace more "democratic."

3) Although the team concept has been introduced, problems with its implementation remain. Namely:
   a. It is not possible to sufficiently motivate individual workers.
   b. Workers cannot be transferred or relocated freely.
   c. There is insufficient awareness of how the team concept can lead to increased productivity and quality.

For these three reasons, we conclude that the team concept has not delivered the results for the Detroit Big Three that it does for Japanese auto companies, whether in Japan or the United States.

In Chapter 4, we describe the accelerated work organization reform carried out at GM following the company's 2009 bankruptcy. Before the bankruptcy, GM plant management had used NUMMI (New United Motor Manufacturing Inc.) and Saturn as models. In the post-bankruptcy period they have attempted to adopt new programs and mechanisms such as continuous improvement, product development teams (PDT), a new labor–management cooperation system, and multiple verification stations as part of the quality control system, while reducing the number of workers.

However, these endeavors sometimes create tension with the UAW. Work organization reforms have been developed thanks to efforts made by both the local union and management. But we observed that Plant A was still struggling to reform its production processes. The first task was to overcome the top-down management style, vertical division of work, job territorialism, and other remnants of traditional American plants. GM plants have been working on various reforms, including improving employee motivation and internal communication, in an attempt to effectively implement lean production. However, this chapter shows that the journey of reform is still ongoing.

Chapter 5 describes GM's Global Manufacturing System, known as GMS. Designed to be a sophisticated and integrated system to innovate the company's work organization, GMS was first implemented at the Eisenach, Germany, plant in 1996 and has subsequently been deployed in GM plants around the world, as well as in suppliers. Work organization reform carried out through GMS has been more effective in improving QCDSM (Quality, Cost, Delivery, Safety, and Morale) than previous reforms were. The UAW and GM have built a strong cooperative system, with UAW–GM Councils at the leadership, operational, and local levels of the company. Covering all GM plants in the United States, these councils are designed to oversee and control the implementation of GMS. This can be said to signify the emergence of new labor–management initiatives.

The following are notable features of GMS.

1) Decreasing the number of job classifications to create a unified wage rate for traditional production workers and expanding the scope of seniority rights
2) Systematically improving the GMS framework
3) Introducing new systems such as verification stations and core teams
4) Establishment of a labor–management consultation system at UAW-represented plants
5) Individual performance evaluation and internal promotion are impossible at this time

Since the 1990s, item 1 of the above list—the introduction of a unified wage rate system for a smaller number of job classifications and expansion of the scope of seniority rights—has progressed. Work on items 2, 3, and 4 began in the early 2000s and accelerated due to GM's bankruptcy in 2009. Achieving item 5, however, has proven to be impossible, and no progress has been made.

Broadly speaking, GM has succeeded in creating a "mechanism" for organization reform (i.e., it has strengthened policy management) for items 1 to 4. In particular, following bankruptcy in 2009, the pursuit of policy management using Toyota's work organization as a benchmark has been formally strengthened. However, the motivation and control mechanisms necessary for implementing it remain weak.

At the time of our most recent survey in August of 2016, there were clearly some operational issues: the PDCA (Plan, Do, Check, Action) cycles were not yet functioning effectively. After the 2015 contract negotiations, the mechanisms for policy management were improved considerably compared to before and could be said to be closer to the work organization system of Toyota, which is the benchmark. GM aims to incorporate key elements of Toyota's work organization system into its own, through GMS and the labor–management consultation system, which resemble those of Toyota. Conducting performance evaluations of union members and promoting production workers to any position above team leader remain impossible. Continued investigation in the future will be needed to evaluate how much progress GM makes in implementing the various organization reforms described above.

Challenges and possibilities of employment relations in the US auto industry: From the viewpoint of Japanese employment relations

In this book we have examined and described the historical evolution and actual conditions of work organization in the US auto industry from the perspective of performance or efficiency management. Most previous research concerning work organization reform in the United States has not taken this perspective; without the perspective of performance management, it is difficult to get closer to and understand the realities of the shop floor. Consequently, while research centered on work organization is still important today, the number of studies on this topic has gradually decreased. As a result of these factors, most previous research tells us little about the actual conditions of work organization in the US auto industry.

Our aim in this book was not to study the work organization of Japanese automakers directly. Rather, we have studied work organization in the

United States and compared it, implicitly and explicitly, with what is known of Japanese work organization from previous research in Japan, including our own. It is obvious that GM often sets targets for improvement based on the performance and quality levels of Toyota and other Japanese automakers. The work organization of Toyota has been employed as a strong "benchmark" for GM.

However, GM and Toyota have very different histories and legacies regarding labor–management relations. While GM uses Toyota as a benchmark, GM also has its own well-developed and time-tested traditions of labor–management relations, as we have described in Chapter 2. This has made GM's path dependency for labor relations different from Toyota's. It follows naturally that actual labor–management relations at GM are unique and different from those at Toyota. This is the reason our research, reported in this book, is needed.

The differences implicit in and created by the different path dependencies of labor–management relations in the two countries are many. They include different ways of resolving conflict and forming a strategy. Japanese automakers have the experience of training and educating blue-collar workers as well as white-color workers and promoting both within the company. Historically, Japanese trade unions accepted a merit pay system in exchange for job security for regular blue-collar workers. Moreover, this job security in Japan is centered on, and granted by, "the company," rather than being based on a job classification. This system of "job security based on the company" is crucial historically and a key to understanding labor relations in Japan.

In the United States, on the other hand, as we have seen in Chapter 2, the UAW has fought hard to achieve job control unionism, in which job descriptions are narrow and detailed and in which seniority plays a very large role. Workers' seniority determines whether they will be laid off or not and when they will be recalled to work. The scope of the seniority rule has been broadened to apply to job transfers and promotions as well. This expansion of seniority-determined job classifications increases opportunities for promotion and transfer within the plant, which protects workers from being arbitrarily laid off by the decision of the foreman. In other words, while there is a job security mechanism called "SEL: Secured Employment Level,"[1] the increase in job classifications is the primary basis for job security for US auto workers. We therefore argue that the United States has a path dependency of "building job security based on job classifications," in contrast to Japan's path dependency of "building job security based on the company."

A fuller study of the nature of labor–management relations in Japan lies outside the scope of this book. However, a thorough account of Japan's labor relations system and how it compares to that of the United States would be valuable. Many researchers have argued that Japanese companies provide job security in exchange for being able to apply a merit pay system to workers in the future. Some researchers insist that in the post-bubble period, Japanese companies can no longer provide guaranteed job security as they have in the past and that they should change to a system of "job security based on job classifications."[2] The principle of "equal pay for the same job" has not been as strongly applied in Japan as in the United States. Especially over the past 20 years, given the intensified international competition, Japanese unions have become increasingly concerned about job security. Discussion of alternate job security systems has increased, but there is still no clear answer for the future.

The purpose of this book is not to predict the future of employment relations in the United States and Japan but to clarify more precisely the historical evolution and actual conditions of work organization reform in the US auto industry. Future dialogue between labor and management should be given close attention in order to understand the future evolution of employment relations in this important industry.

Notes

1 See Chapter 4 of this book; for greater detail also see Ishida and Shinohara (2010), chapter 8.
2 See Kumazawa (1997). Though job security has mainly been based on "the company" in Japan, there have long been debates about the overall employment system in Japan, with job security being among the most important topics.

Reference

Ishida, Mitsuo, and Kenichi Shinohara. (2010). *GM no Keiken*. Tokyo: Chuo Keizaisha.
Kumazawa, Makoto. *Nouryoku Shugi To Kigyou Shakai*. Tokyo: Iwanami Shoten, 1997.

Index

Note: Italicized folios indicate figures and with "n" indicates notes.

Printed in the United States
by Baker & Taylor Publisher Services

Printed in the United States
by Baker & Taylor Publisher Services